LoveWorthFinding
MINISTRIES

Adrian Rogers

"Grace be with you, mercy, and peace, from God the Father, and
from the Lord Jesus Christ, the Son of the Father, in truth and love."

2 John 1:3

GOD'S HIDDEN TREASURES
Biblical Wisdom for the Seasons of Life

A d r i a n   Ro g e r s

GOD'S HIDDEN TREASURES

Biblical Wisdom for the Seasons of Life

Tyndale House Publishers, Inc.
Wheaton, Illinois

Unless otherwise indicated, Scripture quotations are taken from the *Holy Bible*, New Living Translation, copyright © 1996. Used by permission of Tyndale House Publishers, Inc., Wheaton, Illinois 60189. All rights reserved.

Scripture quotations marked KJV are taken from the *Holy Bible*, King James Version.

Library of Congress Cataloging-in-Publication Data

Rogers, Adrian.
    God's hidden treasures : biblical wisdom for the seasons of life / by Adrian Rogers.
        p.   cm.
    ISBN 0-8423-3319-3 (hardcover : alk. paper)
    1. Christian life—Biblical teaching.   I. Title.
BS680.C47R64   1999
242—dc21   99-22150

Printed in the United States of America

04   03   02   01   00   99
7   6   5   4   3   2   1

CONTENTS

INTRODUCTION

Like a finely tuned clock, seasons come and go, easing from summer sunshine to autumn harvests, to wintry snowfalls and spring planting. Over and over through the years, we witness the pattern of birth, growth, rest, and renewal.

God not only governs nature, he nurtures our growth as well. In our life, we experience times of maturing as well as times of dormancy and refreshment. These are the *seasons* of life. Ecclesiastes 3:1 says, "There is a time for everything, a season for every activity under heaven."

Sometimes circumstances give us reason for extreme joy, while at other times we may experience despair like never before. What we do and who we look to throughout these changing seasons is critical to our spiritual vitality.

Focusing on God as Lord of our life is the theme of this book. Only in him can true joy and peace be discovered and maintained. Unearth the treasures of wisdom and inspiration offered within these pages.

May you be blessed by *God's Hidden Treasures: Biblical Wisdom for the Seasons of Life* and encouraged to make the God of the universe the primary focus of your days!

A time to be born and a time to die. A time to plant and a time to harvest. . . . A time to tear down and a time to rebuild. A time to cry and a time to laugh. . . . A time to search and a time to lose. . . . A time to tear and a time to mend. A time to be quiet and a time to speak up. . . . A time for war and a time for peace.
Ecclesiastes 3:2-8

In him lie hidden all the treasures of wisdom and knowledge.

COLOSSIANS 2:3

GOD'S HIDDEN TREASURE

Many, many years ago, the Spanish Armada was sailing off the coast of Florida when a hurricane struck. Those ships, laden with millions of dollars in gold and silver ingots, went to the bottom of the ocean. The treasure had been lost, but no one knew exactly where the ships had gone down.

No doubt fishermen fished near Vero Beach in Fort Pierce, Florida, countless times over the years. They might even have cursed their luck when their lines got hooked on something below — because they couldn't see the lump of gold below them in the water.

Then one day some divers said, "The ships must be around here somewhere." So they dove down into the water and, after only a little searching in shallow water — so shallow that anyone who knew how to swim could have reached it — brought up millions of dollars worth of precious metal. The treasure was found!

Today a great treasure awaits us — a full and glorious life in Christ. If you sometimes feel like the fishermen who missed out on the treasure because they never contemplated what lay below, turn your eyes toward your heavenly Father and his Son, who died for you. As you look in his Word and talk with him, he'll give you discernment so that you can see beyond your earthly hindrances to the treasure of life with him.

He arose, and rebuked the wind, and
said unto the sea, Peace, be still.
And the wind ceased, and there was
a great calm. And he said unto them,
Why are ye so fearful? how is it that
ye have no faith?

MARK 4:39-40, KJV

"Peace, Be Still"

One night Jesus was with his disciples on the Sea of Galilee. Suddenly the wind began to blow, and the sky was filled with lightning. The sea began to churn and boil as the gentle winds turned into a cruel gale, tossing the disciples' fragile ship until it bobbed up and down like a cork on the water.

The disciples looked at one another in despair. Then they turned to Jesus, amazed he was asleep, and woke him up, shouting, "Don't you even care that we are going to drown?" (Mark 4:38).

Jesus said simply, "Peace, be still." And as he said that, the winds ceased, and the Sea of Galilee became as quiet and calm as a baby sleeping on his mother's breast. The moon shone through the storm, and all was quiet again.

This world, dear friend, is headed into a storm, and the spiritual barometer is dropping. Our world will not know peace until Jesus, the Prince of Peace, comes and says, "Peace, be still." But in the midst of chaos, those who have accepted Christ can have a peace that passes all understanding. It comes when we have faith in the all-powerful, faithful one. Have you given your life fully to Christ, who brings peace to your life's storms?

[God] has spoken to us through his Son. . . . The Son reflects God's own glory, and everything about him represents God exactly. He sustains the universe by the mighty power of his command.

HEBREWS 1:2-3

Who Is Jesus?

No one knows the exact date of his birth, yet that event divides all history into B.C. and A.D.

He never wrote a book, and yet more has been written about him than about any other person who ever lived.

He did not earn an M.B.A., a Ph.D., or an M.D. In fact, he had no formal education to bolster his résumé. Yet more schools, colleges, universities, and seminaries have been founded in his name than in the name of any other person ever born.

He's not a painter or composer, but he's been the inspiration for some of the greatest music, art, and poetry the world has ever known.

While he was on earth, he was relatively unknown outside of his own friends and country. He never left his region of birth. Yet never before or since his lifetime has there been a person whose worldwide impact can be felt more—even in our world today.

Who is this extraordinary person? The Lord Jesus—and there has never been another person like him in all of history!

When you wonder, *Lord, am I making a difference in the world at all?* turn your eyes toward Jesus. Look to his example: the love and truth telling he extended to others because he always had their eternal best in mind.

I will show you what it's like when someone comes to me, listens to my teaching, and then obeys me. It is like a person who builds a house on a strong foundation laid upon the underlying rock. When the floodwaters rise and break against the house, it stands firm because it is well built.

LUKE 6:47-48

ANSWERED PRAYER

After a hurricane hit Miami, a woman wrote this letter to the *Miami Herald*, expressing her frustration at how she felt God had "jilted" her:

> *I've never believed in God or in prayer. I thought it was all superstition. But, since the storm was coming, I gave it a try. I asked God to protect my house—but it got damaged anyway. So I just wondered, what do you say about those who say they believe in God and prayer?*

Soon afterward the newspaper printed the editor's response:

> *Madam, I don't know much about prayer either, but I think perhaps God was busy taking care of his regular customers.*

God is not a glorified bellhop running up and down the corridors of heaven, taking orders and trying to impress us with his efficiency in catering to our every whim. Neither is he a sanctified Santa Claus whose sole purpose is to deliver gifts to our door.

None of us is exempt from danger; however, we *are* promised protection amidst the difficulties that come our way from time to time.

If you want God to answer your prayers, submit your life to him as *Lord*. With that submission, God will provide his peace and joy to help you weather *any* storm that might arise.

Give your burdens to the Lord, and he
will take care of you. He will not
permit the godly to slip and fall.

PSALM 55:22

THE GREAT BURDEN BEARER

A man was carrying a heavy load of grain down a country road. Sweat dripped from his brow and soaked his worn shirt, while the dusty air and scorching sun burned his face. A man in a passing wagon noticed his struggle, and, judging the sack to weigh at least fifty pounds, he gently tugged on the reins and slowed his horses. "Mister, you need a ride. Get up here with me, and I'll take you."

Relieved, the tired man climbed up onto the seat and settled in for the remainder of the trip to town. However, he did not remove the loaded sack from his shoulder.

After a moment of silence, the compassionate driver said with consternation, "Why don't you put that down and relax?"

To his surprise, the first man replied, "Oh no! It's enough to ask you to carry me without having you carry this also."

Have you ever done that to God? When you're tempted to carry your burdens by yourself, stop and think about whom you are dealing with. He is *God*—the Creator and Sustainer of the universe! No crisis—whether health, financial, relational, etc.—is a challenge for him, so why handle it yourself?

Our great God offers you his amazing power. Take hold of it today!

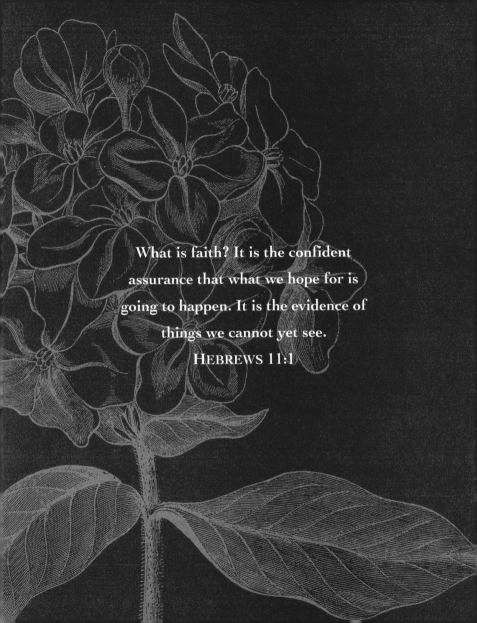

What is faith? It is the confident assurance that what we hope for is going to happen. It is the evidence of things we cannot yet see.

HEBREWS 11:1

TURNING FACT INTO FAITH

While on a recent trip to London, I came across a tiny "virtual-reality" theater. Since I had time to kill before my plane departed, I went inside to check it out.

When the screen came on, Wow! I was on a motorbike, cruising along a mountain path, zooming past towering trees and fallen branches. I zigzagged around obstacles, bounced over stones, and teetered on the tires' edges in an effort to keep the bike upright. Over miles of rough terrain I sped, enjoying the gusts of wind and the thrill of danger.

Then the world went black, and I was back in the airport—a world away from my rugged mountain path. That simulated adventure was so thrilling, I felt disappointed when I realized it was not reality. I had allowed my mind to be fooled.

In real life, we often fall prey to this same fantasy. We believe something to be true just because it seems so wonderful; then we're heartbroken when the dream doesn't turn out as we expected.

But there's one fact you can always believe in and rely on: Christ died for you once, for all time. And if you acknowledge your need for him, he will take you on a journey far more exciting than you ever imagined. He'll turn that fact into faith!

I once thought all these things were so very important, but now I consider them worthless because of what Christ has done. Yes, everything else is worthless when compared with the priceless gain of knowing Christ Jesus my Lord. I have discarded everything else, counting it all as garbage, so that I may have Christ and become one with him.

PHILIPPIANS 3:7-9

The Only Worthwhile Goal

How many of us can honestly say we live moment by moment for Christ, making our quest to know him our priority, believing him to be fully capable of working out his will in our life? What would a life like that look like?

The apostle Paul was an excellent example. His faith *was* his life, and he was confident of his life's purpose. He lived, breathed, worked, suffered, and died for his sole purpose of loving Jesus and helping others come to know the wonderful love Christ offers.

We, too, are to have one primary goal—to know Jesus Christ by *his* definition, not ours. Jesus desires that we seek him personally, powerfully, passionately, and preeminently. That means we love him above our career, our family, our ministry—all things that need our attention.

It's amazing what happens when you focus your life on God. Everything else flows out of that. Everything else contributes to that essential priority of knowing Jesus Christ as *Lord*. If you focus on knowing God first, you can state Matthew 6:33 confidently: "He will give you all you need from day to day if you live for him and make the Kingdom of God your primary concern."

All honor to the God and Father of our Lord Jesus Christ, for it is by his boundless mercy that God has given us the privilege of being born again. Now we live with a wonderful expectation because Jesus Christ rose again from the dead. For God has reserved a priceless inheritance for his children. It is kept in heaven for you.

1 PETER 1:3-4

BLESSED ASSURANCE

Have you ever been on an airplane that flew through a bad storm and been bumped this way and that?

One day a man was on an airplane during just such a storm. In the midst of this crisis, when people's anxiety levels were rising, the man could not help but be amazed by his seatmate's behavior. The petite, older lady seemed to be at ease. In fact, when everyone else was a basket case, she was humming the words to the song "Blessed Assurance."

"Lady," the man queried, "aren't you afraid?"

"Not at all," she replied, smiling confidently. "I'm a Christian. I've given my heart to Jesus Christ." Then, patting his arm gently, she continued, "Not so long ago, one of my daughters died. But because she was a radiantly beautiful Christian, she's in heaven. I have another daughter who's in Denver, where this airplane is going. I'm looking forward to visiting with her. But the truth is, it really doesn't make much difference to me which daughter I visit."

What faith! That woman knew that, as the song says, "Blessed assurance, Jesus is mine! O what a foretaste of glory divine!" She saw herself as just a visitor on earth—rather than as a resident. As you walk through the situations of your day, you, too, can choose whether to be a resident or a visitor on earth. And as you focus more on God while you sojourn on earth, you'll gain even more "blessed assurance" of your life with him in heaven.

God blesses the one who reads this prophecy to the church, and he blesses all who listen to it and obey what it says. For the time is near when these things will happen.

REVELATION 1:3

The Consistency of the Bible

In the Bible, the books of Genesis and Revelation go hand in hand. Genesis, the first book, describes the creation of the heavens and the earth. As the Bible's final book, Revelation deals with the end of this world and the creation of a new one.

The story of the first man, Adam, and his wife, Eve, is vividly told in the early chapters of Genesis. Satan appears for the first time, man is driven from the tree of life, and Paradise is lost. We read of the first death and of humanity's struggle with sin and separation from God. In many ways Genesis sets a grim picture of our future.

How wonderful for us that God chose to end his Word with the glorious Revelation! This book reveals his plan for our return to Paradise. Satan is defeated, never to tempt us away from God again. Jesus and his bride, the church, are united for eternity. In Revelation, God invites all of us to return to his tree of life, where there is no more death.

From beginning to end, the Bible is a thrilling, awe-inspiring book. Open its pages, and enjoy your own personal journey through God's incredible story of grace and redemption to a people desperately in need of him.

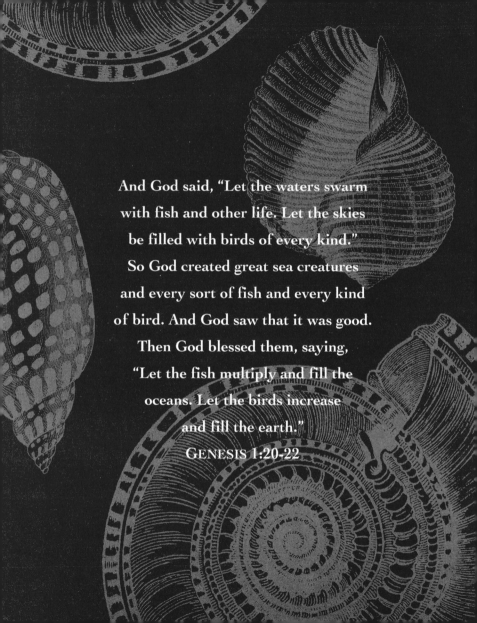

And God said, "Let the waters swarm
with fish and other life. Let the skies
be filled with birds of every kind."
So God created great sea creatures
and every sort of fish and every kind
of bird. And God saw that it was good.
Then God blessed them, saying,
"Let the fish multiply and fill the
oceans. Let the birds increase
and fill the earth."
GENESIS 1:20-22

In the Beginning

An eloquent preacher once said, "God stepped from behind the curtain of nowhere, stood upon the platform of nothing, and spoke a world into existence." God's awesome handiwork is in every minute detail of our world, from the perfection of a tiny amoeba floating in a pond to the intricate network of tiny blood vessels that sustain larger life.

When we stop and ponder the complexity of life—whether it is a forest of towering sycamores, a reclusive sea animal in the ocean's blackest depth, or a squirming baby in a hospital nursery—who deserves the credit? God. In the beginning he made something out of nothing.

Yet many highly educated people claim that our living world happened by chance. But how do they explain the instinctive ability of millions of salmon to determine when they are ready to reproduce, the knowledge to swim miles upstream, and the ability to return to their birthplace to lay their eggs? And what about the yearly pattern of trees—shedding their leaves in the fall, standing dormant through the winter, and waking in the spring to grow a flourish of new leaves?

Evolutionists believe that billions of years, plus chance, can turn frogs into princes. In school they call that a fairy tale. In the laboratory they call it science. Which do you believe?

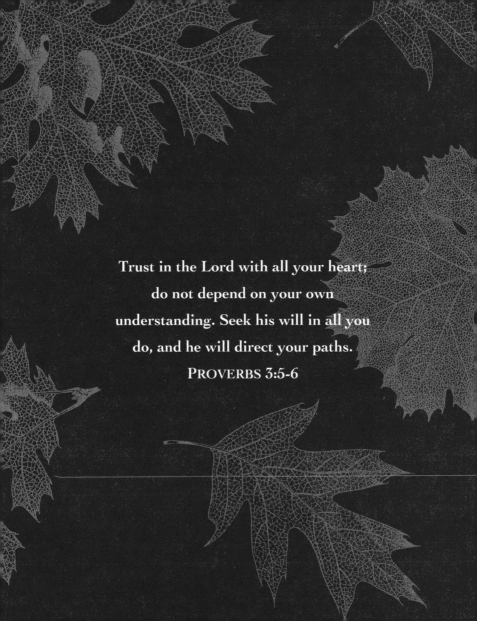

Trust in the Lord with all your heart;
do not depend on your own
understanding. Seek his will in all you
do, and he will direct your paths.

PROVERBS 3:5-6

IT'S WORTH IT

If you knew there was a million dollars in gold buried somewhere in your backyard, what would you do? Probably look for it in a second! You'd be out there spading around for that gold.

Well, God says that if we want to know his will, we must search for his wisdom that way—as if we're hunting hidden treasure. We must have complete confidence in God and in his Word in order to be constantly compliant with his will. In Proverbs 3:5-6, "Trust in the Lord with all your heart" describes complete confidence. "Seek his will in all you do" describes constant compliance. This portion of Scripture is only one of many in which God shows us he wants us to acknowledge him in *all* of our ways—not in just some of them.

God doesn't want a part-time commitment. You can't say, "Lord, I want your will in my social life, but not in my business life" or "I want your will in my church life, but stay out of the rest of the week." God says we are to seek him in *everything* we do, which means we need to turn over every area of our life to him. If he's worth part of it, he's worth all of it.

Jesus said, "Come to me, all of you who are weary and carry heavy burdens, and I will give you rest."

MATTHEW 11:28

AT THE MASTER'S FEET

Once there was a man who had a very well trained dog—a Labrador retriever that loved the water. One day the dog was frolicking in a nearby lake. When it was time to go, the man called the dog, but the animal would not come. The man called several times; the dog would not obey. Finally the man got a stick and threw it out in the water. When the dog saw it, he swam over, got the stick, and came back and laid it at his master's feet.

Have you ever felt as if God has thrown you a "stick"—a broken relationship, the death of a loved one, an illness, a job loss, etc.? God does not cause pain; he allows it. And it just may be that God has allowed you a burden because he, like the master of the Labrador, can't get your attention. It just may be that God has given you a burden so you might come and lay it at your Master's feet.

Today, if your poor heart is aching and breaking, remember the Master—the Savior who loves you. Cast your burdens on him, for he will carry them when you lay them at his feet.

I am the Lord your God. . . . Do not
worship any other gods besides me.
You must never worship or bow down
to them, for I, the Lord your God, am
a jealous God who will not share your
affection with any other god!
EXODUS 20:2-3, 5

WORTHY OF WORSHIP

A story is told of an incredibly gifted concert violinist, Fritz Kreisler, who longed to own a Stradivarius violin. When he heard that an old Englishman had one, he offered to buy it. But the old man said the violin was not for sale.

One day Kreisler ventured to the old man's house, knocked at the door, and asked, "If I can't buy it, may I touch it?"

The old Englishman invited him in and showed him the treasured violin. Kreisler picked up that violin, tucked it under his chin, and began to draw the bow across the strings. As the gifted violinist played, tears began to well up in the old Englishman's eyes and then began to course down his cheeks.

When Kreisler had finished playing and was gazing at the Stradivarius in awe, the old Briton said, "It's not for sale, but it's yours. You are the master and alone are worthy of it!"

Just as there was only one master—Kreisler—worthy of that violin, there is only one Master worthy of worship in our life: Jesus Christ, the Son of God. All earthly things, people, and talents pale in the light of his glory. He alone is worthy of our life's focus and passion.

If you give, you will receive. Your gift
will return to you in full measure,
pressed down, shaken together to
make room for more, and running
over. Whatever measure you use in
giving—large or small—it will be used
to measure what is given back to you.

LUKE 6:38

Planting the Seed

In the very beginning of the world, when God created the herbs of the field, he said, "Let there be trees that grow seed-bearing fruit. The seeds will then produce the kinds of plants and trees from which they came" (Gen. 1:11). And that's exactly what happened. The record continues, "The land was filled with seed-bearing plants and trees, and their seeds produced plants and trees of like kind" (verse 12).

Producing things after like kind happens not only in the plant world but also in the people world! The Bible assures us that everything we do for Jesus, every seed we plant for him, is going to sprout. We may not know it sprouted in this lifetime, but God will use our efforts—even giving a cup of cold water in his name—to impact the world for him.

If you're not reaping the things that you want to reap in life, you may want to consider the seeds you've been planting. In other words, if you want friends, then show yourself to be friendly. If you want people to love you, then start loving people. If you want time, give time. If you want concern, give concern.

The Bible promises us that if we give, we will receive—and the more we give, the more we'll receive!

Whoever pursues godliness and unfailing love will find life, godliness, and honor. If you keep your mouth shut, you will stay out of trouble.

PROVERBS 21:21, 23

Pinpoint Your Problem

Zig Ziglar tells a story about Mr. Sparks, a business executive, who was on his way to the health club when he was stopped for speeding. He was so angry when he got back to the office that he chewed out the sales manager because the sales were down. The problem was, he wasn't really mad at the sales manager; he was mad at the highway patrolman.

Then he talked to his secretary and demanded, "Where are those five letters I gave you? Get those letters out." As a result of her getting yelled at, the secretary went over to the switchboard operator and chewed her out.

The switchboard operator went home that day and found her twelve-year-old son watching television. And, because he had a little tear in his blue jeans, she yelled, "Look, you've torn your pants. Go upstairs — no more TV for you!"

What did the boy do? The cat crossed his path, and he kicked it.

Wouldn't things have been a lot simpler if Mr. Sparks had figured out who he was really mad at — and why — before he took out his anger on someone else? So many times we're hurting in one place and grunting in another. We need to pinpoint our problem before it gets away from us and damages others.

Since God chose you to be the holy
people whom he loves, you must clothe
yourselves with tenderhearted mercy,
kindness, humility, gentleness,
and patience.

COLOSSIANS 3:12

A LITTLE KINDNESS GOES A LONG WAY

A man went into a roadside diner for breakfast. A cranky waitress came out, her hands on her hips, and demanded, "What do you want?"

"Well," the man said, "I'd like some eggs and a few kind words."

Speechless, the waitress just glared at the man and went back to the kitchen. After a few minutes, she came out with a plate of eggs and slapped the mess down in front of him.

Looking first at the eggs and then back up at her, the man asked, "And where are my kind words?"

"Don't eat them eggs," the waitress answered saucily and pranced back to the kitchen.

Everyone—including this man who just wanted some kindness with his breakfast—longs for kind words. A little kindness goes a long way in making an eternal impact for Christ.

A woman once told her pastor, "I've become a Christian because of you."

Overjoyed at the woman's new commitment to Christ, the pastor asked, "Which sermon was it that brought you to Jesus?"

"It was nothing you preached," the woman said. "But I was watching when a woman criticized you to your face. Your kindness convicted my heart. I knew then that what you had was real, so I gave my heart to Jesus Christ."

A person with good sense is respected;
a treacherous person walks a rocky
road. Wise people think before they
act; fools don't and even brag about it!
Only simpletons believe everything
they are told! The prudent carefully
consider their steps.

PROVERBS 13:15-16; 14:15

AN EASY TARGET

Some people are easily fooled. You know the type—they'll believe just about any story you tell them. They're easy targets for Madison Avenue, believing that to "be someone" they need all the glitzy finery in the store window. They're easy targets for the unchristian, antifamily values of MTV and many television shows and movies. When they're invited to church by a friend who's Muslim or Hindu, they think, *Why not? God is everywhere, and I can worship him anywhere—even if I don't believe in their religion.* When a coworker suggests a plan to "make money on the side," they get hooked before they ask enough questions to realize it's an illegal venture.

People who are easy targets live in constant danger of being tricked. They're like children who can be led along if you're holding a piece of candy.

The Bible says we are to be careful—and that we are to evaluate in the light of Scripture every opportunity that's put before us. Is it a godly path? Is it good for us? Is it encouraging to others? Will it lead others to Christ or away from Christ?

For those who are easily fooled, the Bible has some advice: Smarten up, and pray for godly discernment. Don't be an easy target for manipulative people.

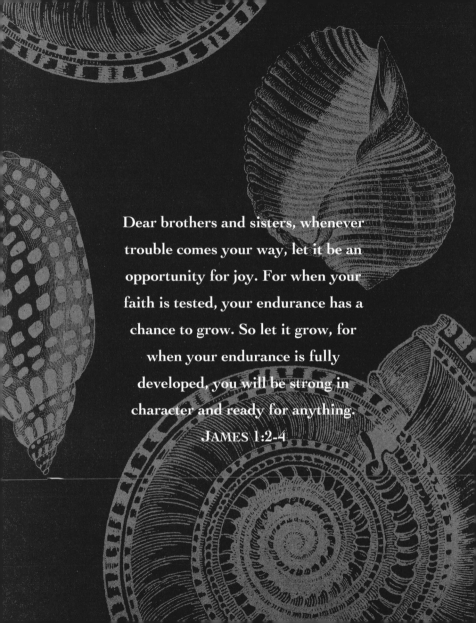

Dear brothers and sisters, whenever
trouble comes your way, let it be an
opportunity for joy. For when your
faith is tested, your endurance has a
chance to grow. So let it grow, for
when your endurance is fully
developed, you will be strong in
character and ready for anything.

JAMES 1:2-4

GROWING UP TO MATURITY

Are children patient? Of course not. Anybody who has had children or worked with children knows that children don't know the difference between "no" and "not yet." For instance, if your child wants an ice-cream cone, and you say, "Not yet. You have to wait awhile—until I get the rest of the errands done," to them you might as well have said no. (This theory has been proven true by the many wails parents have received from backseats as a result of this kind of reasoning.)

But part of growing up, of becoming mature, is learning how to be patient. As the Danish proverb says, "Always give to a child when it cries, and you will have a bad child." Tribulation brings patience, and patience makes us mature.

What does God want out of you? He wants you to be a full-grown Christian. And sometimes, in order to bring you to that full maturity, God allows you to have trials.

The next time you're suffering, instead of getting angry at God for allowing this hardship in your life, thank him for it. Ask him to help you remember that each trouble that comes your way will help you grow up to full maturity in Christ.

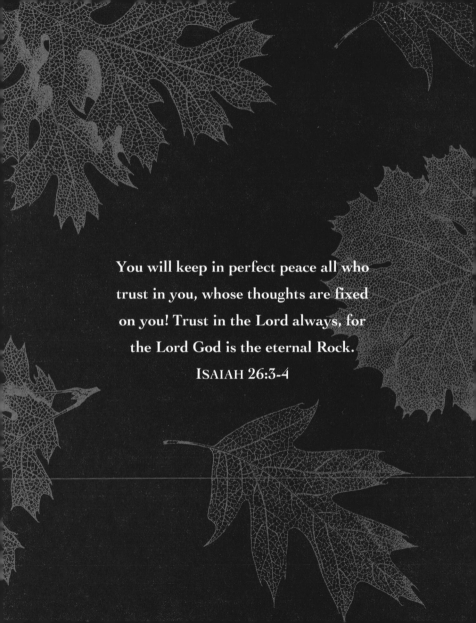

You will keep in perfect peace all who
trust in you, whose thoughts are fixed
on you! Trust in the Lord always, for
the Lord God is the eternal Rock.

ISAIAH 26:3-4

A PEACEFUL CENTER

Because I was raised in the city of West Palm Beach, Florida, where there are so many hurricanes, I learned a lot about these storms. I discovered that in the center of the very worst hurricane, there's a calm spot called the *eye* of the storm. And it's as quiet as a millpond in there.

If you're facing a storm right now that's blowing around you, threatening to knock you and your home down, remember that there is a calm center in the midst of your storm, too. God is there—the peaceful I AM in the "eye" of your trial.

Scripture after Scripture shows us the power and availability of God's peaceful center, even in the midst of our tribulations: "You can live unafraid in peace and safety" (Hos. 2:18); "I am leaving you with a gift—peace of mind and heart. And the peace I give isn't like the peace the world gives. So don't be troubled or afraid" (John 14:27); "You will experience God's peace, which is far more wonderful than the human mind can understand. His peace will guard your hearts and minds as you live in Christ Jesus" (Phil. 4:7).

So, even in tough times, "let the peace that comes from Christ rule in your hearts. . . . And always be thankful" (Col. 3:15).

This same God who takes care of me
will supply all your needs from his
glorious riches, which have been given
to us in Christ Jesus.

PHILIPPIANS 4:19

HAPPILY EVER AFTER?

Most people dream of meeting Mr. or Miss Right—that person who will make us wildly happy the rest of our life. The person who will complement our every talent, want to be with us in every venture, and keep life wonderfully exciting and fulfilling. Because of this innate dream, no wonder so many fairy tales end with "and they lived happily ever after."

But this dream is part of the problem with America today. You see, we think that if we could just find that right person and get married (even if we're already married to someone else), then we'd be happy all the time. All of our needs would be met.

However, the Bible doesn't promise constant happiness. Ecclesiastes, for example, says: "There is a time for everything, a season for every activity under heaven. A time to cry and a time to laugh. A time to grieve and a time to dance" (3:1, 4). What we fail to remember is that no man or woman can make us truly happy. True sufficiency, security, and significance can be found only in our Lord Jesus. If we're looking anywhere else, we're looking in the wrong place—and expecting from a human being what he or she can't humankly provide.

Only God can meet our deepest needs—and lead us to happily ever after.

Teach your children to choose the
right path, and when they are older,
they will remain upon it.

PROVERBS 22:6

Train Up a Child

When a neighbor noticed a little boy riding around and around the block on his tricycle, he got curious and asked, "Son, what are you doing?"

The little boy said, "I'm running away from home."

"But you're just going around the block," the man responded, puzzled.

"Yes. That's because Momma won't let me cross the street!"

Even at his early age, even during his moment of rebellion, this boy was restrained in his behavior because of the training his mother had ingrained on his heart and mind. Today, some believe that children are inherently good and that we should just let them do whatever they want to do. But that's not what God says. His idea of responsibility is very clear: "You yourself must be an example to them by doing good deeds of every kind. Let everything you do reflect the integrity and seriousness of your teaching" (Titus 2:7).

We need to train and discipline our children so they'll become godly adults who bring glory to our Savior. Those who have kids should make sure they not only hold their children accountable but also do the following themselves: "Love the Lord your God, walk in all his ways, obey his commands, be faithful to him, and serve him with all your heart and all your soul" (Josh. 22:5).

Unless the Lord builds a house, the
work of the builders is useless.

PSALM 127:1

BUILDING YOUR HOUSE

It's interesting that those who don't yet have children or work with children have lots to say about how to raise them: "Make sure you put them down to nap at the same time every day." "Don't let them have any candy until they're two." But something mysterious happens when the first little one shows up on your doorstep—all your theories go awry in the face of real-life parenthood. As one preacher said, "Before I got married, I had four sermons on the home and no children. Now I have four children and no sermons!"

Building a godly home is a complicated matter but not an impossible one. However, a home cannot be built by human ingenuity, human wit, and human wisdom alone. What we need is a divine plan, a blueprint—the Word of God—and the divine Builder, our Lord and Savior, Christ Jesus. It's only when our heart is "in tune with" (Ps. 125:4) God, through prayer and the study of his Word, that we have the tools to help build a prosperous, happy, fruitful Christian home.

Have you taken God's standards under consideration in planning your home? Take hold of God's direction and power to make your home a thriving environment.

The path of the upright leads away
from evil; whoever follows that path is
safe. Pride goes before destruction,
and haughtiness before a fall.

PROVERBS 16:17-18

THE PROBLEM WITH PRIDE

Do you get irritated when someone corrects you? Do you accept praise for things over which you have no control, such as a natural beauty, God-given talent, or the place of your birth? When someone harms you, do you just decide, *Well, I can get along without that person. I'm never speaking to him or her again!* Do you find it difficult to seek others' counsel? Do you tend to complain? Do you constantly compare your success to others'? Are you discontent with what you have? Do you want more just because a neighbor has more, and you can't stand that?

If you answered yes to some or all of these questions, you may need an attitude check. A yes answer is an indication of a disease of the human heart called *pride*. The Bible comes down hard on pride, including it in the list of the things the Lord finds unacceptable (Mark 7:20-23).

Instead, God stresses the importance of humility, the opposite of pride: "God blesses those who realize their need for him" (Matt. 5:3). Only when we realize who the holy God is in comparison to who we are will we begin to overcome any problem we might have with pride.

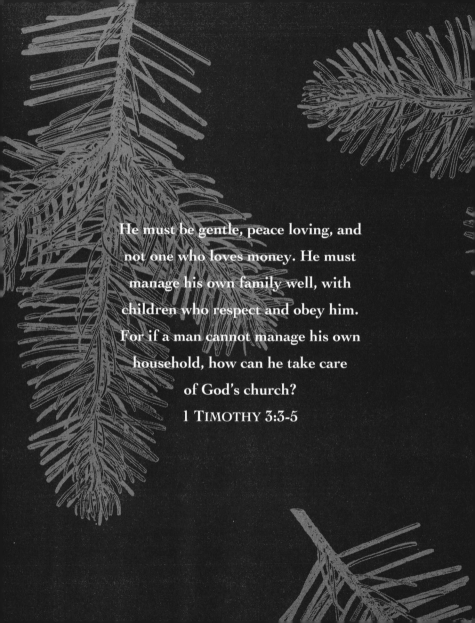

He must be gentle, peace loving, and not one who loves money. He must manage his own family well, with children who respect and obey him. For if a man cannot manage his own household, how can he take care of God's church?

1 TIMOTHY 3:3-5

A GENTLE LEADER

Why is it that we are sometimes the most unkind to those we love the best? The most cutting remarks are often made to a spouse: "What did you do that for?" "I can't believe you're wearing that old thing—again." "You're a slob. Can't you pick up after yourself?"

If only people who are struggling in marriage would realize that the marriage could be saved by a little gentleness—instead of broken by divorce! Both husband and wife are responsible for the condition of their relationship, but let me speak for a moment to the male half of the marriage partnership.

The key to being a great leader is to be gentle and peaceable. In 1 Timothy, the apostle Paul describes the character of a church elder, whose godly qualities are also beneficial in the home. He must be "a man whose life cannot be spoken against. He must be faithful to his wife. He must exhibit self-control, live wisely, and have a good reputation" (3:2).

If you want your marriage to be great, practice gentle leadership. Encourage with your words, instead of nitpicking or showing insensitivity. Be kind, building up your wife, instead of saying things that will make her angry (see Prov. 15:1).

As Matthew 5:5, 9 says, "God blesses those who are gentle and lowly. . . . God blesses those who work for peace, for they will be called the children of God."

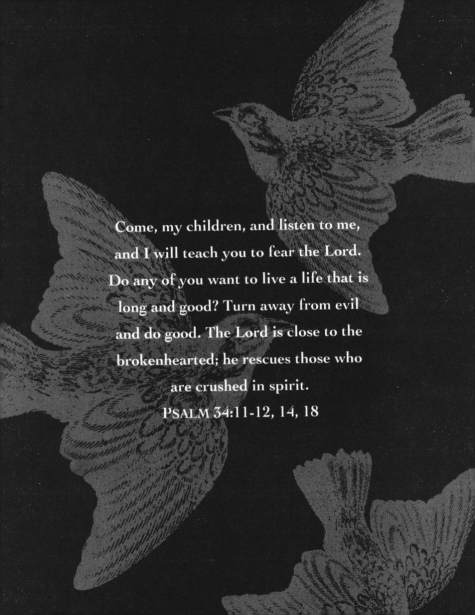

Come, my children, and listen to me,
and I will teach you to fear the Lord.
Do any of you want to live a life that is
long and good? Turn away from evil
and do good. The Lord is close to the
brokenhearted; he rescues those who
are crushed in spirit.

PSALM 34:11-12, 14, 18

A Repentant Heart

When a child disobeys his parents, do you know what that child has done? Yes, he has sinned against his parents, but what's more, he has sinned against God.

If you want your child to learn the truth of Ephesians 6:1 — "Children, obey your parents because you belong to the Lord, for this is the right thing to do"—then you need to talk to your children when they sin. Say, "Listen. Daddy's and Mommy's hearts are broken because you did that. You know why? Because God doesn't want us to behave that way."

So many parents fail by disciplining a child because of their own anger. They just want to punish the sin instead of working for the child's repentance toward God. Although you can't act as the Holy Spirit in your child's heart, *making* him repent, you can *pray* for that repentance. You can *explain* why what your child did was so wrong before God.

After the punishment is over, make sure you "receive" your child. Give him or her a hug, and kiss away the tears. Never hold grudges. Learn to be firm, to be fair, and always to point the way toward God. Let your kids see God at work in your home through a repentant heart.

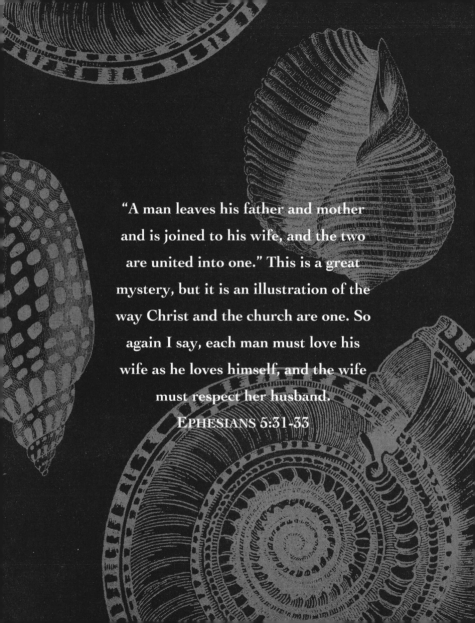

"A man leaves his father and mother and is joined to his wife, and the two are united into one." This is a great mystery, but it is an illustration of the way Christ and the church are one. So again I say, each man must love his wife as he loves himself, and the wife must respect her husband.

EPHESIANS 5:31-33

PRIORITY CHECK

Marriage is not a happenstance. It was the first institution built by almighty God; it was divinely established by the Creator for the protection and development of humankind's deepest physical, psychological, emotional, and spiritual needs: "Since they are no longer two but one, let no one separate them, for God has joined them together" (Matt. 19:6). Therefore, the marriage relationship is the supreme human relationship.

What does this mean? That your relationship to your spouse should come before your business. That your relationship to your spouse should come before your friends. That your relationship to your spouse should come before your own personal pleasure.

The Bible teaches that when one man and one woman come together at the marriage altar and consummate the marriage act, they become one flesh, not to be put asunder. Marriage is not a ninety-day option; it's a lifetime contract.

That means I am to love my wife passionately—with the emotion and commitment that come from the deepest part of my being. And she is to do likewise. We are to be each other's highest love on this earth apart from the Lord Jesus.

You must commit yourselves
wholeheartedly to these commands I
am giving you today. Repeat them
again and again to your children. Talk
about them when you are at home and
when you are away on a journey, when
you are lying down and when you are
getting up again.

DEUTERONOMY 6:6-7

A WONDERFUL OPPORTUNITY

People are always asking, "Pastor, how do we teach our kids about the Bible? How do we go about family worship?"

Although setting time aside for family prayer and worship is important, let it be brief. Oh, there will be times when your kids want to know more and start asking questions. You might talk for hours. But don't frustrate your children by making them sit still for a long period of time.

So many of us have the idea that Bible instruction is "You sit still while I instill." It's like trying to force your kids to take a dose of cod-liver oil once a day—and having to ram it down their throats.

Instead, be creative. Be like Jesus, who saw everyday objects and events as opportunities to teach. For instance, he used salt (Matt. 5:13), light (Matt. 5:14-16), birds (Matt. 6:26-27), lilies (Matt. 6:28-30), someone knocking on the door (Matt. 7:7-8), and bread and fish (Matt. 7:9-10).

Teaching the Bible ought to be as normal as eating, breathing, walking, sitting, and rising. How many wonderful ways there are to teach your children! Are you taking advantage of the day-to-day objects in your home and on your travels—and the events that you share—to teach your children about God?

The commandments of the Lord are right, bringing joy to the heart. The commands of the Lord are clear, giving insight to life. Reverence for the Lord is pure, lasting forever.

PSALM 19:8-9

Taking Advantage of the Whys

It's the fifth time in less than twenty minutes that your child has yanked on your jeans and asked, "But why, Mommy?" By now your nerves are ragged because you have so many things to do—other than answer your little one's constant questions.

But consider this: Children have a natural, God-given instinct to ask *why*. They're intellectual sponges, just waiting to soak up God's truth. It's well documented that when a child is young, the curiosity factor is high. So is the memory factor, the humility factor, and the trust factor. What better time for us to begin training our children to be godly?

When kids are young, we have the greatest opportunity to shape them to be straight, strong, balanced arrows that can pierce their world. As the psalmist says, "Children are a gift from the Lord; they are a reward from him. Children born to a young man are like sharp arrows in a warrior's hands. How happy is the man whose quiver is full of them!" (Ps. 127:3-5).

The next time your toddler insistently asks you why, instead of getting frustrated, try training with a tidbit here, a tidbit there. Then sit back, and watch that child listen and absorb a godly lifestyle.

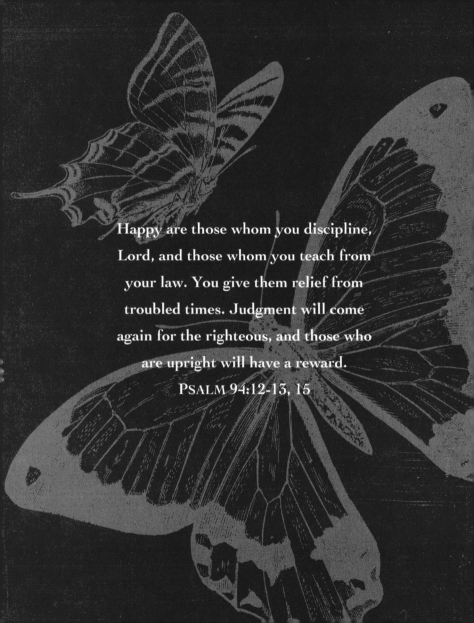

Happy are those whom you discipline, Lord, and those whom you teach from your law. You give them relief from troubled times. Judgment will come again for the righteous, and those who are upright will have a reward.

PSALM 94:12-13, 15

THERE'S SECURITY IN LIMITS

All of us long for security—to know where we stand with those we love, to know that someone cares deeply for us in return. And no one longs for that more than your children.

If you want to be a good parent, you have to set limits. Yes, your child will test those limits, but do you know why? He wants to know if you love him enough to say, "No! I will not allow you to do that, because I love you and because God loves you." If you don't hold firm on your limits, your child loses his sense of security. When limits change, there's no safety, and children don't know what to expect. They're not sure whether you'll punish or reward them for their actions, whether you'll let them get away with it this time but not next time.

One of the worst mistakes a parent can make is setting no limits on a child. Why? Because a child senses no limits as rejection and thinks, in essence, *My parents don't care whether I come in late with the car or not;* or, *They don't love me enough to follow through with discipline for my bad behavior.*

If you don't establish boundaries for your child, someone else will—and that person might take advantage of him or her. Have you set loving limits so your child feels secure?

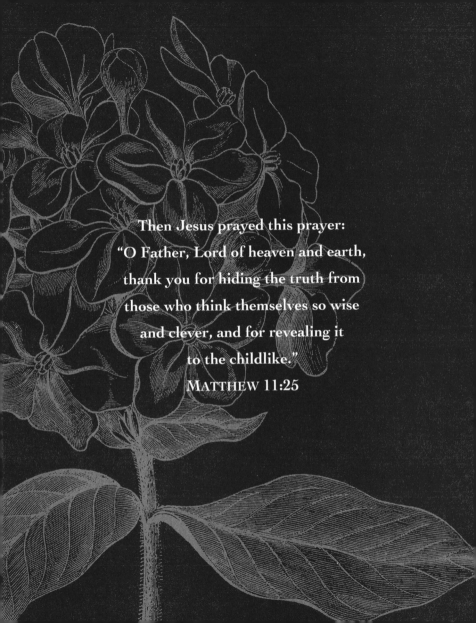

Then Jesus prayed this prayer:
"O Father, Lord of heaven and earth,
thank you for hiding the truth from
those who think themselves so wise
and clever, and for revealing it
to the childlike."

MATTHEW 11:25

THE FAITH OF A CHILD

Parents often ask me, "At what age are my children accountable for their faith? When can they understand what being a Christian really means?"

Don't ever get the idea that little children cannot believe in Jesus Christ. They can. In fact, Jesus says in Matthew 19:14, "Let the children come to me. Don't stop them! For the Kingdom of Heaven belongs to such as these."

The main thing to watch for is this: Is the child aware that he is a sinner—not just that he's done some bad things? Is she aware that our righteous and holy God has to punish sin? If the child knows these things and can verbalize them (even in simple language), it's time to point that child to Jesus.

But be careful you don't push a child prematurely. You wouldn't want to vaccinate your child with a mild form of Christianity so that the real thing may not be effective later. Your responsibility is not to block that child's early faith, nor to shove faith on him or her, but to guide.

When you sense the Holy Spirit's conviction, pray for discernment, then present the Lord Jesus. Ask if your child would like to receive Christ in his or her life. And thank God for his working in your child's heart!

No one can serve two masters. For you
will hate one and love the other, or be
devoted to one and despise the other.
You cannot serve both God
and money.

MATTHEW 6:24

What's Mastering You?

A man of modest income once said to a very rich man, "I have more than you have."

Startled, the rich man replied, "How is that so?"

"Because I have all I want, and you don't," the other man said.

It's true—the more wealth you have, the more you worry about it's being taken away or being enough. Here's just one example. If you watch television, you may be familiar with a show from some years back: *Lifestyles of the Rich and Famous*. I've often thought the program actually should have been titled *Lifestyles of the Rich and Foolish*.

The people featured on the show may have had a fleet of cars, a lavishly decorated home (or several homes), wardrobes bursting with expensive shoes and clothing, and a vault heavy with jewels. But those things don't equal happiness. They often create a desire to seek after more and more in order to be fulfilled. As Solomon, the wisest man who ever lived, said, "I collected great sums of silver and gold, the treasure of many kings and provinces. But as I looked at everything I had worked so hard to accomplish, it was all so meaningless" (Eccles. 2:8, 11).

A healthy attitude toward money is one of the first elements of good priorities.

A prudent person foresees the danger ahead and takes precautions; the simpleton goes blindly on and suffers the consequences. Listen to the words of the wise; apply your heart to my instruction. In this way, you may know the truth.

PROVERBS 22:3, 17, 21

TAKING SIN SERIOUSLY

A Christian television and film writer attended a producers' conference. While attending a workshop led by one of TV's most successful sitcom producers, the Christian was shocked. That successful producer stated his sincere conviction that in order for a TV script to be commercially successful, it must violate at least three of the Ten Commandments.

Friend, if that's what TV producers think—and the answer is obvious if you watch many of the programs—then we as Christians need to get some channels off our television sets altogether.

In my estimation, one of the most dangerous things on television is the sitcom. Why? Because it's getting you to laugh at sin. And what you laugh at you don't take seriously.

If you're a parent and you allow a television into your house, you need to sit down and watch the programs your children watch, especially if they're young. Discuss what you see, and help them learn to evaluate how what they're seeing stacks up against the truths of the Bible. As Hebrews 8:10 says, "I will put my laws in their minds so they will understand them, and I will write them on their hearts so they will obey them."

What have you been filling your mind with lately? Do you take sin as seriously as God does?

They [the Jewish religious leaders] called the apostles back in and told them never again to speak or teach about Jesus. But Peter and John replied, "Do you think God wants us to obey you rather than him? We cannot stop telling about the wonderful things we have seen and heard."

ACTS 4:18-20

OBEYING GOD FIRST

What would you do if the government decreed that you couldn't pray in public or attend church anymore?

Many people throughout the world have faced such a decision. Those who've continued to pray and attend church have faced tremendous persecution—even death.

In Moses' early days, when the pharaoh of Egypt demanded all boy babies be killed, the godly midwives refused to do it—knowing it was man's law and not God's. This story is even more poignant to us today, since hospitals are now performing abortions, and Christians have to decide whether or not to work there.

Young Daniel was another person who chose to obey God rather than people. Carried as a slave from Jerusalem into Babylon, Daniel refused to bow to the social and political pressure of that pagan nation. He would not acknowledge the Babylonian gods, nor would he pray to the Babylonian king. Daniel wasn't shy about saying the Israelite God was the only God he would follow. As a result, he was thrown into the lions' den. However, much to the Babylonians' shock, God showed his almighty power and delivered him.

The Bible makes it clear that the church is not the servant of the state. It is the conscience of the state. We must be civil in our Christian beliefs, but we cannot be silent.

Whenever we have the opportunity, we
should do good to everyone, especially
to our Christian brothers and sisters.

GALATIANS 6:10

A GOLDEN OPPORTUNITY

Do you remember the story of the Good Samaritan? He was on a journey and spotted a bruised, bleeding man by the side of the road. This Samaritan—a person the Jewish leaders considered "lower class" because of his heritage—didn't make excuses as the others who passed by previously had. He didn't say, "I'm too busy" or "I'm on a journey, and I don't have time." He didn't say, "It's really none of my business."

Instead, that Samaritan stopped in his tracks and set about helping the man as best he could. It was a golden opportunity to help a fellow human being, and the Samaritan took it.

Today, there are bruised and bleeding people all around us. Some are bleeding financially, others emotionally. Many are bleeding spiritually. These hurting people need Christians who will stop long enough in the road of life to say, "This is a golden opportunity, and I'm going to take it right now."

How true it is that the chief enemy to kindness is busyness. We're all busy. We have our to-do lists, our jobs, our family duties, our church responsibilities, and we feel overwhelmed. But if we're too busy to be kind, then we're too busy.

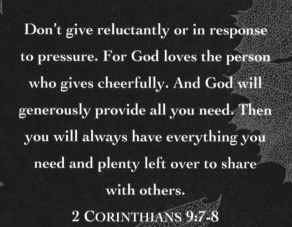

Don't give reluctantly or in response
to pressure. For God loves the person
who gives cheerfully. And God will
generously provide all you need. Then
you will always have everything you
need and plenty left over to share
with others.

2 CORINTHIANS 9:7-8

A GENEROUS GIVER

Mr. DiVensenzo, a PGA golfer, won a tournament. Just as he was handed a check, a woman showed up. "Please, sir, my baby is dying."

His heart touched, Mr. DiVensenzo endorsed the check and gave it to the woman on the spot. "Take this, and try to buy some happiness for yourself and for the child." Then he got in his car and drove off.

A week later, when he was in the clubhouse having lunch, one of the PGA officials approached him. "You know that woman to whom you gave the check?"

DiVensenzo nodded.

"Well, she doesn't have a sick baby. She's a phony."

"You mean there's no baby dying of an incurable disease?" DiVensenzo asked, surprised.

"That's right," the official said.

"That's the best news I've heard all week," DiVensenzo stated emphatically.

What a godly attitude that PGA golfer had! He could have felt ripped off by the woman. But instead, he felt grateful that he had been given at least the opportunity to save a human life.

You know, some of us have grown cynical. We're so afraid that someone is going to take advantage of us that we don't give to the truly needy when we should. But the Bible leaves it up to God to even the score score and simply says, "Give generously to others in need" (Eph. 4:28).

Always be full of joy in the Lord. I say it again—rejoice! Don't worry about anything; instead, pray about everything. Tell God what you need, and thank him for all he has done.

PHILIPPIANS 4:4, 6

JOY FOR ALL TIME

What if you came home and found out your house had been burglarized? Your jewelry, your mementos, your TV, your microwave, even your car in the garage was gone. Worse than that, the perpetrators had burned your house to the ground. Would you still have joy?

If you got all your joy from your house and its furnishings, I doubt it. You'd just stare in shock at your charred, ruined life.

What if tragedy struck—a child died, or your spouse was diagnosed with an incurable illness? If you got all your joy and security from your human relationships, I doubt you'd have any joy left. You might sink into a deep depression.

However, if your joy is in the Lord, you'd still have it—no matter what the circumstances. You see, the Bible never says rejoice in your house or rejoice in your furniture or rejoice in your automobile. What it says is rejoice in the Lord! It's important to remember that happiness is fleeting—it's an outside job. But joy is forever—it's an inside job.

When your joy comes from the Lord because he is enthroned in your heart, that joy is permanent—it can never be taken away. Do you have the Lord's joy deeply embedded in your heart?

It is the Spirit who gives eternal life.

Human effort accomplishes nothing.

And the very words I have spoken to

you are spirit and life.

JOHN 6:63

Restoring Hope

Back in the 1950s, many young people "lost their innocence." Ironically, they lost their freedom by being "liberated" by music, films, automobiles, money, and education.

In the 1960s times got worse. The youth of that day rebelled against every authority figure—their parents, teachers, the church, and the government. The result was that they were left with nothing to believe in.

In the 1970s our youth lost their hold on the definition of true love and settled for sex—a poor substitute for our human longing for commitment to one person for a lifetime.

The 1980s and 1990s further catapulted this loss of innocence, authority, and love until today's teens don't know what—if anything—to believe in. Life is lived on the spur of the moment, and excitement is the catchword of the day. Why is that so important? Because today's youth have lost hope and they're looking for excitement to fill the meaningless days. As a result of this liberalism, many of these young people don't know where they are headed.

The only hope for today's culture is a restoration of hope—found in the Word of God. Anything you can do to help the children and teens of today get involved in a church that preaches and teaches the Word of God could make a mountain of difference in America's future.

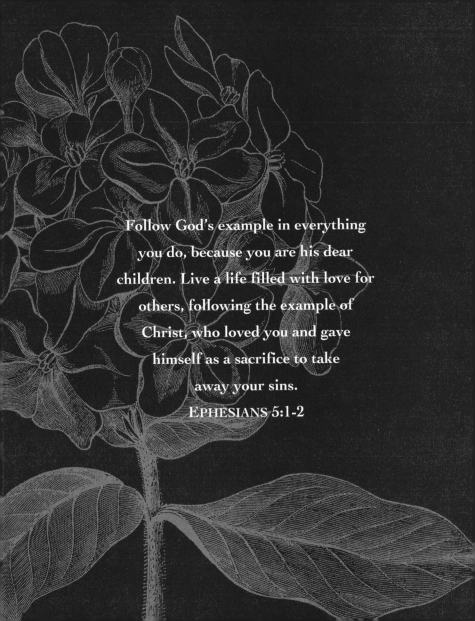

Follow God's example in everything you do, because you are his dear children. Live a life filled with love for others, following the example of Christ, who loved you and gave himself as a sacrifice to take away your sins.

EPHESIANS 5:1-2

Loving as Christ Loved

When a little boy was looking through his family's picture album, he came across a picture of his mother just after his mother and father had been married. Surprised that his mother once looked so young, he asked his dad, "Daddy, is that when Mother came to work for us?"

Sadly, many people think that when the Bible says a wife is to submit to her husband, they think that means the husband is a little lord, and the wife is to wait on him. "Would you like some more coffee, honey?" "May I bring you your slippers, honey?"

But that's not what the Bible teaches. That's not the way Christ loves the church. He gave himself to us—even dying on the cross for our sins—as a sacrifice.

What most marriages deeply need today are two funerals and a wedding: when the husband and the wife die to themselves, they are married to each other. Only then can husband and wife begin to live sacrificially, giving themselves to one another.

The Bible makes it clear that the husband, if he loves his wife as Christ loves the church, is going to love her sacrificially.

Kiss me again and again, for your love
is sweeter than wine. How fragrant
your cologne, and how pleasing your
name! . . . Take me with you. Come,
let's run! Bring me into your bedroom.
SONG OF SONGS 1:2-4

OUR DEEPEST NEEDS

Do you want your marriage to be more exciting and fulfilling? Then here's a key truth you should learn: There's a difference between men and women. Women are lovers; men are achievers.

The Bible says in Ephesians 5:33, "Each man must love his wife as he loves himself, and the wife must respect her husband." Why is there a different command for husband and wife? Because God knows the difference between man and woman. God tells the man to love his wife. God tells the woman to respect her husband. Why does God use those commands? Because he knows our deepest needs.

If asked to name a woman's deepest need, most women would probably give this answer: Romance. They want to be loved, cherished, and prized. They want to be held, adored, and put on a pedestal. They want to be No. 1 in your parade. They want to be loved.

What do men say is their greatest need? To be admired. To be respected.

When you look at God's commands through that lens, you realize that he's known from the beginning our deepest needs. Why not trust him more fully by following his plan for your love relationship with your spouse?

Salvation that comes from trusting Christ—which is the message we preach—is already within easy reach. . . . For if you confess with your mouth that Jesus is Lord and believe in your heart that God raised him from the dead, you will be saved.

ROMANS 10:8-9

To Believe Is to Trust

John G. Patton was a missionary to the South Sea Islands. When on a particular island he encountered people who did not have the gospel translated into their language, he set out to do just that. When he came to the word *believe,* which doesn't mean merely head belief or intellectual belief, he searched for a word that the natives would understand. He wanted them to know that *belief* in Christ also meant commitment and trust, but he couldn't seem to get across the right word.

One day, as Patton was in his room writing, a native arrived to deliver a message. Since the man had run from the other side of the island, he was out of breath. He sank down into a big chair in Patton's room, simply leaned back, and relaxed.

Startled and thrilled, Patton realized a connection. So he asked the native, "What were you doing? Give me the word." When the native gave him the word for what it meant to sit down in a chair, relax, and put your weight upon that chair, Patton penned in that word for his translation of "believe."

My friend, that's exactly what believing means: that you quit trying, begin to trust in the Lord Jesus, and relax in his arms.

For all have sinned; all fall short of
God's glorious standard. Yet now God
in his gracious kindness declares us not
guilty. He has done this through
Christ Jesus, who has freed us by
taking away our sins. . . . We are made
right with God when we believe that
Jesus shed his blood, sacrificing
his life for us.

ROMANS 3:23-25

WINGS OF GRACE

Many of the 6 billion people on this earth are busy doing good work—feeding the hungry, caring for children, making advances in medicine that will curb disease. And yet, even if you could extract from each person the best character trait and put all those traits into one person, that one person would still have to bow humbly before God and cry out for mercy to be saved. Even the best of us break the Ten Commandments. How incredible, then, that Jesus came to earth as the ultimate sacrifice for our sins—to bring the gracious gospel to us in human form.

The Old Testament law says, "Do this and thou shalt live." The New Testament gospel says, "Live, and then thou shalt do." The law says salvation is wages; the gospel says salvation is a gift. The law demands holiness; the gospel provides holiness. The law says run, but it gives us no legs. The gospel says fly, and it gives us wings of grace.

With the focus in today's world on work—that you have to *do* something important to be worthy or valued—it's difficult sometimes to believe God doesn't want our work. He wants our heart. Are you busy trying to earn your salvation? Or have you truly accepted God's free, unmerited gift of grace?

He issued his decree to Jacob; he gave his law to Israel. He commanded our ancestors to teach them to their children, so the next generation might know them—even the children not yet born—that they in turn might teach their children. So each generation can set its hope anew on God.

PSALM 78:5-7

Sowing and Reaping

If you want to be depressed, listen to the news. I once heard about a baby who was born addicted to drugs as the result of his parents' habit. The parents had sown that seed, and the little child was reaping the bad results of their behavior. The news report added that statistics showed if the child did not get help, he, too, would grow to have drug-dependent children. How true the Scripture is that says the sins of the parents are visited on the third and fourth generations (see Exod. 20:5)!

But the good news is that the reverse is also true. Jesus said in John 4:36-38, "What joy awaits both the planter and the harvester alike! You know the saying, 'One person plants and someone else harvests.' And it's true. I sent you to harvest where you didn't plant; others had already done the work, and you will gather the harvest." In other words, we can reap where we haven't sown. As long as we are willing to sow the seeds of Christ's love and truth, we will have a good harvest. It may not be in this generation, but it could be in the next.

How positively wonderful it is to know we *can* sow for others. We can be a blessing for generations to come!

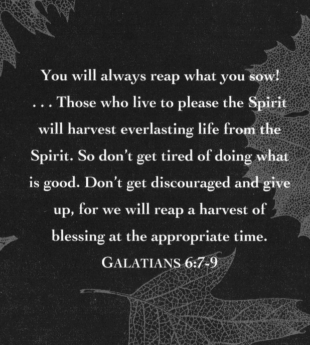

You will always reap what you sow!
. . . Those who live to please the Spirit
will harvest everlasting life from the
Spirit. So don't get tired of doing what
is good. Don't get discouraged and give
up, for we will reap a harvest of
blessing at the appropriate time.

GALATIANS 6:7-9

CULTIVATING YOUR HARVEST

Have you ever planted a garden and thought, *Oh, how beautiful it is—I can't wait to see the fruits, vegetables, and flowers!* Then you went on vacation—and returned to weeds. Everywhere.

That's a fitting analogy for our life today. There is a good harvest—our growing life in Jesus Christ and the ability we have to point others toward God—but often that harvest is choked out by thorns, weeds, and briars. Because we live in a sin-cursed world, there's even more reason to cultivate our soil after we plant the seeds.

For instance, every time you have a quiet time, you're weeding the garden of your mind so the good seed of God's Word can multiply. And when you pray throughout the day, asking God's help for patience with your children or an angry coworker, you're watering your garden.

What are your harvests—the resulting fruits, vegetables, and flowers of your spiritual life? When you go out to win souls, when you talk with your coworkers, neighbors, relatives, or friends about Christ, the Bible says you'll reap a harvest of blessing.

In what ways do you need to weed or water your garden today? With whom could you share the harvest of your life in Christ?

Dear brothers and sisters, you must be patient as you wait for the Lord's return. Consider the farmers who eagerly look for the rains in the fall and in the spring. They patiently wait for the precious harvest to ripen. You, too, must be patient. And take courage, for the coming of the Lord is near.

JAMES 5:7-8

THE LAW OF THE HARVEST

Anyone who's visited Sequoia National Forest in California has gazed upon the giant sequoias in awe. Some of them are three hundred feet tall—that's the height of a thirty-story building. Some have trunks thirty feet in diameter, and some live up to four thousand years! Yet each of these giant trees began with the smallest of seeds. Then, through time, that seed began to grow and mature until it became a full-grown tree.

The same thing is true of our spiritual life. It begins as a seed of faith and then grows as we mature. As we serve God in small ways, he begins to give us even bigger ways to serve him. But we must never forget that this is a slow process. Sometimes it may feel as if we're not growing at all; yet under the surface, our growth can be steady.

If you feel discouraged by your slow growth and wonder if you're making a difference in others' lives, consider the growth of the sequoia. It takes a long time to get to its full awe-inducing size, but what glorious splendor when it finally does!

We need to keep in mind that the best harvest can't be hurried. We must be patient as we wait for God to grow us up to be more like him. God's law says that, in due season, you *will* reap.

I have this complaint against you. You don't love me or each other as you did at first! Look how far you have fallen from your first love! Turn back to me again and work as you did at first. Anyone who is willing to hear should listen to the Spirit and understand what the Spirit is saying to the churches. Everyone who is victorious will eat from the tree of life in the paradise of God.

REVELATION 2:4-5, 7

Turning Up the Heat on Lukewarm

How much do you *really* love Jesus? Do you set aside special time to spend with him? Do you follow him as much now as you did when you first met him? Are you as eager to share with others about his love and your changed life?

If your answer is no, you may be feeling lukewarm about your faith. However, feeling lukewarm is more than just "the spiritual blahs." In essence, lukewarmness is saying, "God, I believe in you, but you don't excite me anymore. I don't have that warm, loving feeling about you that I used to have. You're not that important to me."

The church at Ephesus was lukewarm, and God's charge against that church in the book of Revelation was scathing: he said they had left their first love. It wasn't that they didn't love the Lord Jesus—they just didn't love him like they used to.

Reflect honestly. Have *you* left your first love? If there ever was a time when you loved Jesus more than you do at this moment, your honest answer should be yes. And if that's your answer, ask God to turn up the passion of your faith from lukewarm to hot as you dig in to the Scriptures to reveal his words to you. (See Rev. 3:15-16, 19.)

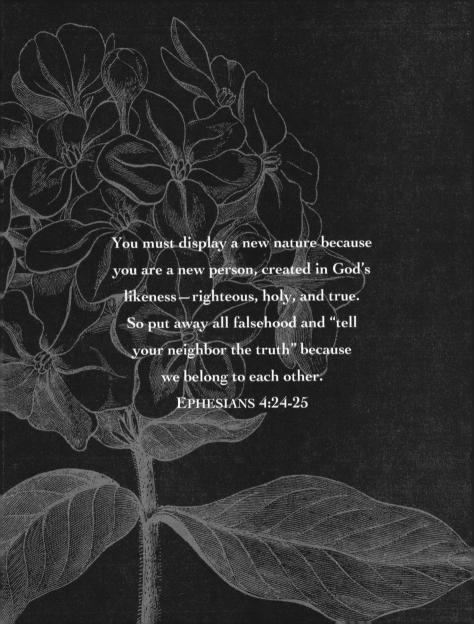

You must display a new nature because
you are a new person, created in God's
likeness — righteous, holy, and true.
So put away all falsehood and "tell
your neighbor the truth" because
we belong to each other.

EPHESIANS 4:24-25

TELLING THE TRUTH

When I was in college, I pastored a little church 130 miles away from school. Every weekend I'd drive the almost three-hundred-mile round-trip in my old rattletrap automobile.

One particular Sunday night, I realized one of my headlights was burned out. But I started back to the college anyway.

When the highway patrolman stopped me, I immediately knew why. Sure enough, as I got out of the car, he asked, "Son, did you know one of your headlights is out?"

Wondering what to say, I finally blurted out, "One of my headlights is out?"

Taking my answer to mean I did not know, the patrolman shook his head and said, "Son, you'd better get that fixed."

"Yes, sir," I replied and got back into my car. But as I continued to drive, the Holy Spirit convicted me. *Adrian, you lied.*

I argued, *No, I didn't. I just repeated what he said.* Yet I couldn't get away from the Holy Spirit's conviction to tell the truth—the whole truth, and nothing but the truth.

Are there areas in your heart and life that are not based on impeccable truth? If so, you've given the devil a foothold. It's time to tell the truth!

The Lord God said, "It is not good for the man to be alone. I will make a companion who will help him."

"At last! Adam exclaimed. "She is part of my own flesh and bone! She will be called 'woman,' because she was taken out of a man." This explains why a man leaves his father and mother and is joined to his wife, and the two are united into one.

GENESIS 2:18, 23-24

A LOVING ACCEPTANCE

Have your spouse's faults ever driven you crazy? In such times, here's food for thought: the Bible says that a husband is to love his wife as Christ loved the church. What does that mean? Total commitment.

When I fail, Jesus doesn't say, "So long, Adrian. You blew it, and I want a divorce. I no longer want to be your Lord. I'm finished with you." No! My Lord stays with me and says, "Never will I leave you. Never will I forsake you." He continues to walk alongside me, even in my failure, because he's committed to my best interest for the long haul.

You say, "But what about my mate's faults? How can I put up with them over the long haul?" The best way is to accept them. No one is perfect; you have faults, too. Then think about the flip side: your spouse's character failures may actually be God's gift to you in order to help you develop a godly character. For instance, your spouse's constant lateness may be God's gift to help you develop patience.

Above all, remember that God knows what he's doing. And he also has a great sense of humor—good thing, since he made us! If we're patient enough to take the long view, that action will go a long way toward loving acceptance and unity.

I tell you, use your worldly resources to benefit others and make friends. In this way, your generosity stores up a reward for you in heaven.

LUKE 16:9

A TEST OF FAITHFULNESS

What would you do if you had a million dollars—cold cash, taxes paid?

Some of us have the best intentions: "Oh, I'd give to the poor, and I'd set aside money for college. I'd pay off my house and buy my mother a car. I'd give more than 10 percent to the church."

But would you really? Here's the best test of what you would do with a million dollars: it's what you're doing right now with that hundred dollars you have in your pocket or bank account. The Bible tells us that it's by learning to be faithful with the little we have that we'll truly be faithful when God blesses us with more talent or a larger sum of money. If we can't use what we have wisely, how can he trust us to control more?

In God's kingdom everything we do and are, are a part of everything else we do and are. For instance, if we aren't faithful with our finances and in helping others, we may not feel God's hand of blessing on us spiritually.

How are you doing with the "little" you have—financially, spiritually, talentwise? What can you do today to be faithful so that, in due time, God may honor you with more responsibility in his kingdom?

Sing a new song to the Lord, for he has done wonderful deeds. He has won a mighty victory by his power and holiness. The Lord has announced his victory and has revealed his righteousness to every nation!

PSALM 98:1-2

Praying with Confidence

One night a little boy was up late reading a murder mystery. It involved a dastardly villain who plotted all kinds of mayhem for the heroine. After a while the boy couldn't stop shivering in dread. He felt so sorry for the heroine—and he became so afraid of the villain himself—that he couldn't stand the suspense any longer. Instead of waiting to finish the book, he decided to skip to the last chapter. When he found out the villain got his comeuppance at the end of the book and the heroine was delivered, he sighed with relief. Relaxed and certain of the end, he could go back and read the remainder of the book. But this time his attitude was different. Every time the villain would plot another evil deed, the boy would say, smiling, "If you knew what I know, you wouldn't be so proud and cocky right now." You see, he had read the last chapter.

Friends, as God's children, we already know the last chapter of this life. We know how the story of good and evil is going to end. Satan, the ultimate villain, will get his comeuppance—for eternity. Therefore, we can pray with confidence to our God, knowing he has all situations under his control. He has already won the victory!

Jesus Christ is Lord, but you cannot have what he gives eternally unless you accept *who* he is.

For we are not our own masters when we live or when we die. While we live, we live to please the Lord. And when we die, we go to be with the Lord. So in life and in death, we belong to the Lord.

ROMANS 14:7-8

COMMITMENT OR SURRENDER?

While preaching in Romania, I had the honor of sharing an automobile ride with Joseph Ton—a leader in the great revival that has been sweeping Romania. During our time together, I asked him, "What problems do you believe are part of the American church and 'American' Christianity?"

His reply was thought-provoking. "Adrian, in America, the key word of the Christian faith seems to be *commitment*." After a long pause, he continued, "If you look in the Bible, the key word God uses is not *commitment*; it's *surrender*. And there's a big difference in philosophy between the two."

How right this godly man's comment was. If we truly long to become God-honoring Christ followers, we cannot just make a commitment. If we do, we are, in essence, holding on to the control; we are choosing the commitment, not choosing Christ himself. Instead, we must surrender to the Lord Jesus Christ—to his way, to his plan for our life. We must truly consider him Lord.

Have you merely "committed" to Jesus' way, or do you treat Jesus as *Lord?* Have you taken that step of surrender?

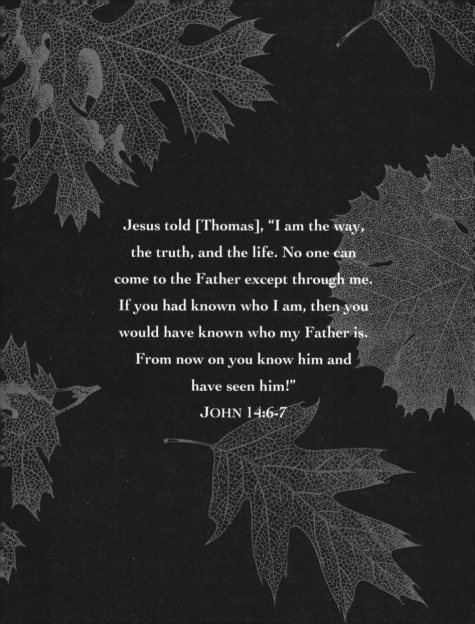

Jesus told [Thomas], "I am the way, the truth, and the life. No one can come to the Father except through me. If you had known who I am, then you would have known who my Father is. From now on you know him and have seen him!"

JOHN 14:6-7

Only Jesus

Today's world is full of "ways out." Take one look at your television, the billboards dotting the highway, and advertisements on the Internet, and you'll be bombarded with messages of materialism. When all else fails, the world says, "Buy your way out."

Other examples abound. Politicians lobby for campaigns that will "legislate our way out." The United States Army tells you to be all that you can be and learn to "fight your way out" of any situation. And the millions of Americans who work long hours believe they can "work their way out." Philosophers spend long hours "thinking their way out"—and then telling us we can do it, too!

But in the Christian life, the Bible makes it plain there's only one way out—through Jesus Christ. If you want to go to heaven and be assured of your eternal future, Jesus, God's Son, will save you by grace—all by himself. There's nothing you can do to earn it. Your good works cannot save you. Your money cannot save you. And here's the flip side: your badness is not enough to keep Christ away. All you have to do is accept him.

Jesus loves you. He stands waiting to save you instantly so that you can enjoy heaven forever with him. What a glorious, freeing truth!

Worship Christ as Lord of your life.
And if you are asked about your
Christian hope, always be ready to
explain it. But you must do this in a
gentle and respectful way. Keep your
conscience clear. Then if people speak
evil against you, they will be ashamed
when they see what a good life you live
because you belong to Christ.

1 PETER 3:15-16

OUR STEADFAST HOPE

Our contemporary culture is filled with those who think Christians are weak people who use God as a crutch. The media plays up Christians who have "fallen from grace." Coworkers scoff at employees who pray over their lunch. But *are* Christians mere fools or sentimentalists—or do we have reasons for believing in the Lord Jesus Christ?

My dear friend, I've learned that "religion" without Christ will never satisfy the hungry heart. If you go to Confucius's tomb, you'll find it occupied. If you go to Buddha's tomb, he'll be there as well. But if you go to the tomb of Jesus, you'll find it empty. He is a *risen* Savior—and the Bible records the eyewitness accounts!

It's been said that you can take Confucius out of Confucianism and still have Confucianism. And you can take Buddha out of Buddhism and still have Buddhism. But you cannot take Jesus Christ out of Christianity and still have Christianity. Why? Because Christianity is not a code, a creed, or a cause. It's Christ himself, living in you.

Jesus alone takes the sting out of sin, the pain out of parting, the gloom out of the grave, and the dread out of dying. Jesus alone gives a hope that is steadfast and sure.

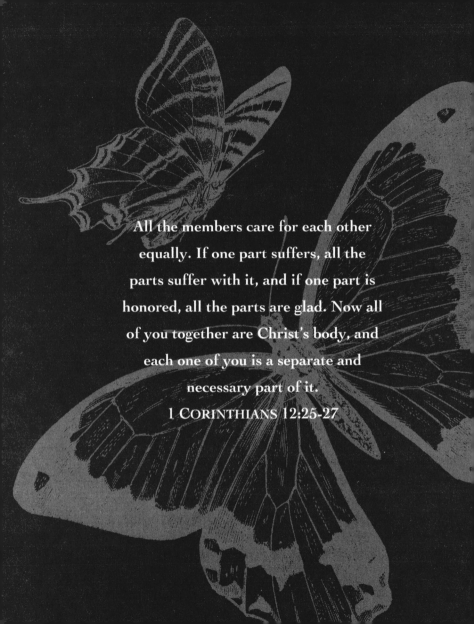

All the members care for each other equally. If one part suffers, all the parts suffer with it, and if one part is honored, all the parts are glad. Now all of you together are Christ's body, and each one of you is a separate and necessary part of it.

1 CORINTHIANS 12:25-27

A New Perspective on Suffering

As long as people live on the earth, they will ask this question: *If there is a God, why is there so much suffering?* Some will decide, *Maybe he has the power to remove suffering, but he just doesn't care.* Others may think, *Maybe there is a God, and he really does care. He wants to take away our suffering, but he doesn't have the power.* Still others conclude, *Maybe there's no God at all.*

Why *is* there so much suffering in the world? The Bible makes it clear, beginning with the book of Genesis. You see, the universe has a disease called *sin,* and God cannot remove our pain until the last vestige of sin is gone. If God took away the pain that he allows as a consequence of our sin, our world would be paradise, and we would have no need of heaven. We would never come to God.

But God doesn't leave us adrift when we suffer. He says he's continuously with us. And what's more, the Bible speaks about the body of Christ, stating that when one member suffers, every member suffers. Without pain and sorrow in life, we would be so independent that we'd miss out on the abundant blessings of being part of God's community.

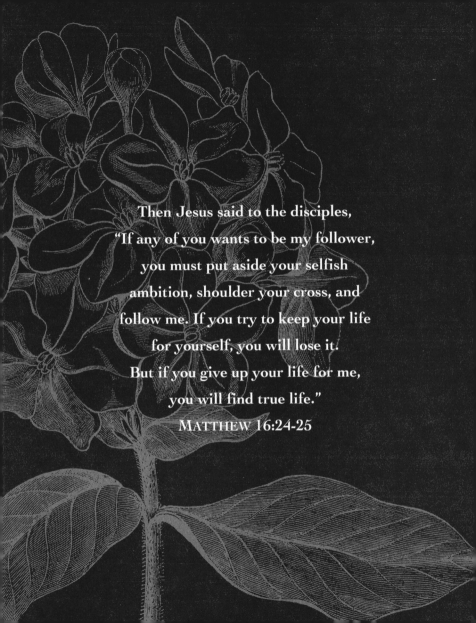

Then Jesus said to the disciples,
"If any of you wants to be my follower,
you must put aside your selfish
ambition, shoulder your cross, and
follow me. If you try to keep your life
for yourself, you will lose it.
But if you give up your life for me,
you will find true life."

MATTHEW 16:24-25

STANDING UP FOR CHRIST

Dr. Criswell tells the story of a beautiful Dallas debutante who was also a talented pianist. Life was easy for this young woman with an exceedingly wealthy father until the day the finger of God touched her soul. With tears she gave her heart to Jesus Christ. But when she went home and told her father, this businessman flew into a rage. He told her angrily, "I will give you time to renounce your faith."

The next morning, the girl walked softly but confidently down the spiral staircase from her bedroom and approached the piano. Without hesitation she began to play and sing these words: "Jesus, I my cross have taken, all to leave and follow Thee; destitute, despised, forsaken, Thou, from hence, my all shalt be." Stunned, her father watched in silence for a moment. Then, with tears streaming down his cheeks, her dad said, "My precious daughter, if the Savior means that much to you, I need him, too." And he gave his heart to Jesus as well.

How about you? Do you stand up for Christ? Can others see him in your life, in your actions, in your priorities? As someone once said, "If a court had to decide from just the evidence of your life whether you are a Christian or not, would they be able to?"

No, dear brothers and sisters, I am still
not all I should be, but I am focusing
all my energies on this one thing:
Forgetting the past and looking
forward to what lies ahead, I strain
to reach the end of the race and
receive the prize for which God,
through Christ Jesus,
is calling us up to heaven.

PHILIPPIANS 3:13-14

PRESSING AHEAD

In his time, Ty Cobb was one of the greatest baseball players in the game. Ty was best known for stealing bases. The crowds would go wild as they watched this talented man make good on run after run.

Yes, Ty held the record for runs scored. But he also struck out many times. Yet this great player didn't let his failures discourage or stop him; he pressed ahead.

And that's exactly what we need to do in the Christian life. Instead of assessing ourselves as a "failure" in a certain spiritual area, why not face our faults, do our best to fix them, then forget them and move ahead? If we fix our eyes on the goal of heaven and our eternal life there instead of our failures in this present life, we won't become as discouraged.

Friend, remember that failure in the Christian life is not final. Our God is a God of victory over failure!

Happy are those who have the God of
Israel as their helper, whose hope is in
the Lord their God. . . . He is the one
who keeps every promise forever.

PSALM 146:5-6

BEING A PROMISE KEEPER

Through talks with teenagers, I've discovered that many of them hold a tremendous amount of bitterness and anger toward their fathers. Why? Over and over I've heard the refrain: "Because he never keeps his promises. I can't count on him." Their dads promise to be at a football game, then never show up because of mounting paperwork at the office. Or they miss a family dinner because they had to meet a business client. The message promise breakers are really conveying to their kids is this one: *You're not as important to me as other things*.

So, dads, if you want to restore your relationship with your teenager, the best thing you can do is remember and then list those times when you broke your promises. Talk to your child, using the list, and share your genuine remorse. Be vulnerable—ask that child to list other times when you've failed to keep your promises. At last, tell your child that you've asked God to forgive you for breaking your word, and now you're asking for your child's forgiveness.

But make sure your action doesn't end there. True repentance means you turn around and go the other way. Become, in your future interactions, a promise keeper your family can trust!

Just as our bodies have many parts and each part has a special function, so it is with Christ's body. We are all parts of his one body, and each of us has different work to do. And since we are all one body in Christ, we belong to each other, and each of us needs all the others.

ROMANS 12:4-5

UNITY IN THE BODY

Have you ever heard of a left hand wanting to be a right hand? Or a right hand wanting to be a left hand? Of course not, because both hands are members of a unified body. The right hand cannot direct the left hand, and the left hand cannot direct the right hand. Both hands have to receive instruction from the head in order to work properly. In other words, they have to *submit* to the head—otherwise the right hand and left hand would be fighting each other to get anything accomplished!

In the same way, the church of Christ is also a body. All of us are members of the body, and, like the left hand and the right hand, we play different roles. God put us in a body together so we might submit to each other out of fear of the Lord, who is the Head of the body.

Do you struggle with submitting to fellow believers? Do you sometimes wish you could be a left hand instead of a right hand? Never forget what Matthew 19:30 says: "Many who seem to be important now will be the least important then, and those who are considered least here will be the greatest then." Every part of the body of Christ is important—including you!

Dear brothers and sisters, if another
Christian is overcome by some sin, you
who are godly should gently and
humbly help that person back onto the
right path. . . . Share each other's
troubles and problems, and in this way
obey the law of Christ.
GALATIANS 6:1-2

RESTORING A BROTHER

As a youngster raised in West Palm Beach, Florida, I loved to collect coconuts and sell them to tourists. One day I had shimmied up a thirty-foot-tall coconut tree. Just as my right hand disconnected a coconut, the palm frond let go. Most of my body landed on the grass underneath the tree, but my left arm smashed onto the sidewalk.

It was bad. My arm was mangled, with a compound fracture. My brother, who was with me, saw what happened and rushed over to my prone form.

As I was lying there, having fallen so low, what did I need? I certainly didn't need a lecture from my brother. I didn't need for him to tell the neighborhood, "Hey, did you hear what Adrian did?" And I certainly didn't need him to come along and shoot me to put me out of my misery. What I needed was restoration—a helping hand to get me home and then to the doctor to repair my brokenness.

In the same way, when a member of our church—a brother or sister in Christ—falls into sin, he or she needs our helping hand. And it's our solemn responsibility before almighty God to restore such a one.

Do you help—or shoot or gossip about—the wounded in your church?

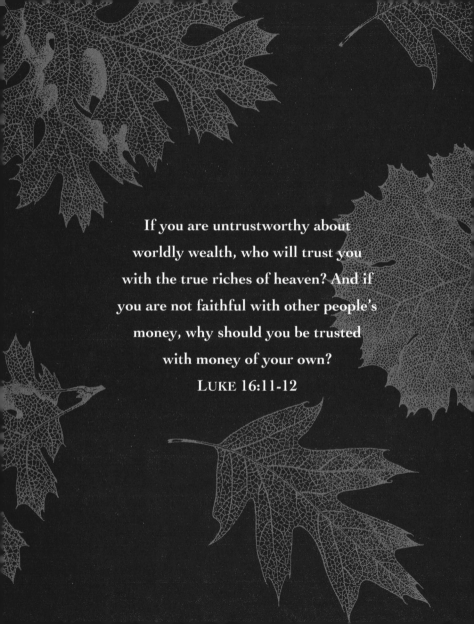

If you are untrustworthy about worldly wealth, who will trust you with the true riches of heaven? And if you are not faithful with other people's money, why should you be trusted with money of your own?

LUKE 16:11-12

A Faithful Steward

Did you know God may be withholding a blessing from you?

For instance, maybe God allowed you a high income, but you've squandered so much of it on a huge house (to impress your colleagues) and too many fine clothes (to make others jealous) that you don't have any funds left to give to the church. Or, on the flip side, perhaps God led you to an inexpensive property where you could build a home large enough to house needy people, yet when you finished the house, you decided that you didn't "feel" like sharing your home, because it was messy and hard work.

If we are not faithful with the resources God gives us (earthly provisions), how can we expect him to shower us with spiritual blessings (heavenly provisions)?

What are true godly riches? Here are just a few: insight into the Word of God, knowing that God listens and answers our prayers, fellowship with Jesus Christ—the God-man who understands us, joy unspeakable even through the tough times, realizing that this world is not the end but that we have the glory of heaven awaiting us! No matter what your earthly finances look like, you can have all these lasting riches. But God calls you to be faithful with what he's given you first.

Make the most of every opportunity
for doing good in these evil days.
Don't act thoughtlessly, but try to
understand what the Lord wants you
to do. . . . Let the Holy Spirit
fill and control you.

EPHESIANS 5:16-18

PRAYER DOES CHANGE THINGS

God is really good at pointing out when you're wrong—even when you don't want to admit it.

One day my wife, Joyce, and I were disagreeing over an issue. We were sitting at the kitchen table, and it was getting tense. Finally she said, "Adrian, you're wrong."

"No, I'm not," I retorted.

"You *are*," Joyce insisted, "but I can't prove it, because you can word things better than I can. But that doesn't change the fact I know you're wrong."

Indignantly I got up and went into my study to try to prepare a sermon. But I couldn't do it. Finally I gave up and started praying instead: *Lord, did you see what went on in there? Can you believe how wrong she is?*

You're the one who's wrong, a quiet voice replied. It stunned me. After thinking about the issue, I realized God—and my wife—were right. I *was* wrong, and I went out to seek my wife's forgiveness.

It's amazing how being honest with God through prayer allows you to hear what God is saying to you. If you keep prayer at the forefront of your life and relationship, you'll have a marriage that will stay committed through any confrontation because it's sheltered by God's great love.

Be on guard. Stand true to what you believe. Be courageous. Be strong. And everything you do must be done with love.

1 CORINTHIANS 16:13-14

LEADING BY LOVE

Unfortunately, many men get the idea that because the Bible says they are to be the head of the home, they are to *make* their wives do this and that.

But let me ask you a question: Has Jesus Christ ever *made* you do anything? Has he ever *made* you pray? Has he ever *made* you give to the church? Has he ever *made* you witness to your neighbor? The answer is no—certainly not. And yet he's the head of the church! That's because Jesus knows that when we force someone to do something, that person will not respond out of love but out of bitterness or fear.

How many marriages could be changed if husbands realized it is not their job to force their wives into submission? Their job is to lead lovingly, not to treat their wives as inferiors and themselves as superiors. If a man is not leading his wife lovingly, he's not treating her as Christ treats the church.

That means husbands should show their wives more love, tenderness, and patience. They should try to be a little more romantic—because that's what brings women pleasure.

Husband, are you leading by love—or by force?

Be careful! Watch out for attacks from the Devil, your great enemy. He prowls around like a roaring lion, looking for some victim to devour. Take a firm stand against him, and be strong in your faith. Remember that your Christian brothers and sisters all over the world are going through the same kind of suffering you are.

1 PETER 5:8-9

RESPECTING THE DEVIL

There is a problem with the way people treat the devil.

Some people treat him carelessly and flippantly, as a joke. Laughing, they picture him as a feisty, red-horned little man. By all the nicknames they call him, it's clear they're not taking him seriously.

Others focus too much on him—they're always studying, wondering, and talking about demons. Their focus is on Satan rather than on the Lord Jesus. They actually chase after the devil, looking for a demon under every bush.

But the biblical approach to how we should treat the devil is vastly different. The Bible says we need to recognize that we have an awesomely powerful adversary. The apostle Peter compares him to a roaring lion who is ready to grab and devour us at any minute. A mature Christian acknowledges that he or she has a strong enemy and respects that powerful enemy—but he or she also follows the Bible's mandate to resist the devil, calling upon God for help.

Yet in the midst of our struggle with the enemy, we can be assured of this promise: "In his kindness God called you to his eternal glory by means of Jesus Christ. After you have suffered a little while, he will restore, support, and strengthen you, and he will place you on a firm foundation" (1 Pet. 5:10).

His unfailing love toward those who
fear him is as great as the height of the
heavens above the earth. He has
removed our rebellious acts as far
away from us as the east is
from the west.

PSALM 103:11-12

REAL VS. FALSE CONVICTION

If you don't learn the difference between Holy Spirit conviction and satanic accusation, you'll be a miserable Christian.

When the Holy Spirit convicts you of a sin, he's specific: "You told a lie"; "you exaggerated the truth"; "you were selfish"; "you were filled with pride"; "you disobeyed me"; or "you've been missing your quiet time." The Spirit puts his finger right on the sore spot and pushes so that you can identify what you've done wrong. This is legitimate or "real" conviction.

On the other hand, Satan just wants you to feel bad or discouraged in general so that you'll be a defeated Christian (or even choose to walk away from God because of your disappointment). And if making you feel awful in general doesn't work, he pulls out an old trick—he accuses you of some sin in the past that has already been forgiven.

Friend, if you've placed your sin under the blood of Jesus Christ and asked forgiveness for it, then that sin is gone—as far away from you as the east is from the west. So if your sin keeps popping up to haunt you, be assured it's not God bringing it up!

If this happens to you, claim Jesus' authority over the power of the enemy: "Satan, in the name of Jesus, I resist you. Be gone."

Look! I am about to cover the earth with a flood that will destroy every living thing. Everything on earth will die! But I solemnly swear to keep you safe in the boat, with your wife and your sons and their wives.

GENESIS 6:17-18

A FIRM HOLD

Sometimes when people give their testimonies about how God has changed them through a crisis, they end by saying, "Pray for me, that I will hold on to the end."

Imagine if the Noah of the Old Testament had had that view. I can just see him, with his wife and family, holding on for dear life to the slimy pegs on the outside of the ark as the water rose. And Noah, seeing the floodwaters come closer to the bottom of his tunic, says, "Honey, pray for me—that I'll hold on to the end." He never would have made it through the storm-tossed floodwaters!

But that's not what the Bible says. It says God said to Noah, "Come into the ark." Thank God that he did! And when Noah came in, God shut the door. He locked Noah and his clan safely in, and the waters, out. He didn't expect Noah to cling to the outside of the boat with exhausted fingers; he provided a way to keep Noah safe.

No matter the situation, God doesn't ask us to hang on with our fingernails. Although it's important for us to be faithful, it's more important that we realize God is the one who has a firm hold on us, who keeps us safe through any floodwaters.

Unless you are faithful in small matters, you won't be faithful in large ones.

LUKE 16:10

WHY SMALL THINGS AREN'T REALLY SMALL

Did you know that all big things are really made of little things?

For example, your body has various members—and these members have various parts, which have smaller components called cells, which are made up of molecules. And as vast as the ocean is, it's made up of drops of water, which are made up of molecules, which are made up of atoms, etc.

The list could go on and on. Sometimes it's easy to look at the little things in our life and think, *Well, it really doesn't matter if I show up for Sunday school today. No one will miss me*. Or, *If I just stretched the truth here, it would keep me out of trouble financially. And no one would know.*

But, just as your body and the vast ocean are made of lots of little parts, so is your life. The big things in life—whom you marry, what job you pursue, the depth of your relationship with Jesus Christ—are determined by your day-to-day decisions.

Are you faithful in the little things, little acts, little words, and little thoughts of your day? If you are, you don't need to worry about the big things.

Nothing in all creation can hide from him. Everything is naked and exposed before his eyes. This is the God to whom we must explain all that we have done.

HEBREWS 4:13

SECRETS REVEALED

A story is told about the famous Italian sculptor, painter, architect, and poet Michelangelo when he was painting the Sistine Chapel. One day he was working way up in a corner, out of everyone's view, when someone told him, "Forget that corner. Nobody else can see the work you're doing there." Michelangelo interrupted his work to make his view clear: "I know that, but I also know this: *I* know it's there. And I also know that what you are in secret is what you are. Nothing more and nothing less."

How much better many of us would fare if we held tightly to that same philosophy! For instance, what about the people who travel a lot and feel lonely in a hotel room? They flip on the television, can't find anything to watch, then spot the R-rated and X-rated movie offerings. They think, *Well, nobody would know if I just watched one....* But those individuals are wrong—Jesus is in that room.

My friend, who you are when you are alone—when your spouse, children, friends, colleagues are not there—is who you really are. Do you need to make any changes in your life so that you don't have to fear your secrets being revealed?

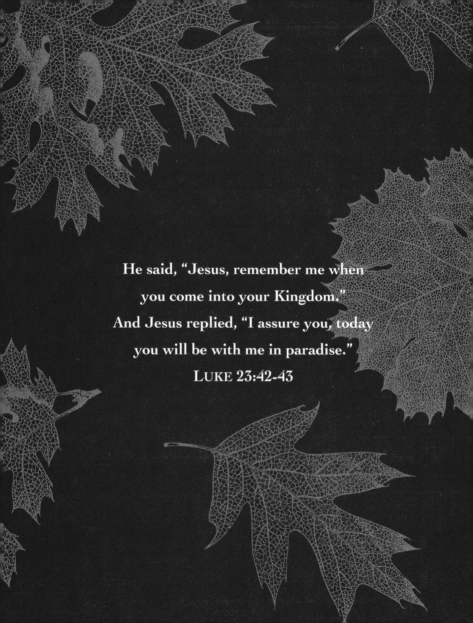

He said, "Jesus, remember me when
you come into your Kingdom."
And Jesus replied, "I assure you, today
you will be with me in paradise."

LUKE 23:42-43

A TRIP TO PARADISE

When a man named Mr. Solomon Peas died, he had these words chiseled on his tombstone: "Beneath these clouds and beneath these trees lies the body of Solomon Peas. But this ain't Peas—it's just the pod. Peas shelled out and went to God." I like that!

Solomon Peas knew our body is just the pod—nothing more. And that view is confirmed by Scripture passages such as 2 Corinthians 5:1: "We know that when this earthly tent we live in is taken down—when we die and leave these bodies—we will have a home in heaven, an eternal body made for us by God himself and not by human hands."

What happens to a person who has trusted Christ as his personal Savior? First Corinthians 15:54-55 tells us: "When this happens—when our perishable earthly bodies have been transformed into heavenly bodies that will never die—then at last the Scriptures will come true: 'Death is swallowed up in victory. O death, where is your victory? O death, where is your sting?'"

When a Christian closes his eyes in this life, he opens them in the next. Jesus did not say, "After two or three thousand years, you'll be with me in paradise." Jesus said, "Today you will be with me in paradise."

The wicked perish and are gone, but the children of the godly stand firm.

PROVERBS 12:7

THE INTEGRITY PAYOFF

The board of a company had talked for a long time about a certain employee—about moving him up to be one of the company's chief executives. It would be a monumental advance for the man, worth thousands of dollars.

Then one day in the company cafeteria, the CEO just happened to be behind this man in line. He saw that man take a pat of butter, worth about three cents, and hide it under a slice of bread on his tray so the cashier wouldn't see it.

That afternoon, the CEO went back to the board and told them they had the wrong man in mind—that this man didn't have integrity. Although the man had no idea the CEO was right behind him, he lost thousands of dollars and a high position—all because of dishonesty over a three-cent pat of butter.

Numerous Scriptures point out the importance—and rewards—of integrity, including: "If you do these things, your salvation will come like the dawn. Yes, your healing will come quickly. Your godliness will lead you forward, and the glory of the Lord will protect you from behind" (Isa. 58:8) and "It is better to be poor and godly than rich and dishonest" (Prov. 16:8).

Do you live and act with integrity in every area of your life? If your CEO, Jesus Christ, were behind you in line, would he be pleased with your actions?

You have been born again. Your new life did not come from your earthly parents because the life they gave you will end in death. But this new life will last forever because it comes from the eternal, living word of God.

1 PETER 1:23

The Ultimate Authority

Many centuries ago an emperor named Diocletian reigned over the Roman world. He so hated the Bible that he ordered all Bibles confiscated and destroyed. He also ruled that Christians who claimed the name of Jesus be put to death, many of them with excruciating pain. This man hated Christianity so intensely that he once personally burned a Bible and erected a monument on top of it. The following words were chiseled on the marker: *Extincto Nomini Christianorum,* which means "The Name of Christian Is Extinct."

However, in spite of Diocletian's effort, he couldn't keep the truth of the Bible from revealing itself and from changing lives and nations. The name of Christ did not become extinct. In fact, in A.D. 325 Constantine enthroned the Bible as the infallible judge of truth in the first general church council.

Even this one historical anecdote—and there are thousands upon thousands—is enough to confirm what the Bible itself says about being the incorruptible Word of God. Nothing—time, people, politics—can destroy the solid foundation of the Bible. Throughout all time, its manuscripts have been protected against error. And no other historical document has been proven so true—even against scientific and medical evidence.

We can count on the lasting truth of the Bible. It is our ultimate authority, and we should treat it as such.

The word of God is full of living power. It is sharper than the sharpest knife, cutting deep into our innermost thoughts and desires. It exposes us for what we really are.

HEBREWS 4:12

CHANGED BY THE WORD

I've been preaching the Word of God for over four decades now. And I still never fail to be astounded by what takes place when you preach the gospel, tell the truth, and pray for wisdom and discernment in how to approach people with the message of Christ. There's something supernatural that takes place: People's lives are radically, dramatically, eternally changed through the Word of God. Isn't that wonderful?

When you preach the Word of God from the pulpit or share it with your loved ones and neighbors one-on-one — without stuttering, stammering, apologizing, or trying to tweak its clear message — the words of Scripture cut through any pretense, lie, or excuse. They're like a white-hot cannonball ripping through paper.

There's power in God's Word — and that's why Satan does everything in his power to block your understanding of the authority of the Bible. Satan knows well that once you accept the Bible as your authority, he and his angels will have to flee from you on all sides.

Have you stood firm on the power of the Word of God? Do you treat it as the ultimate book that has changed your life?

You put us in charge of everything you made, giving us authority over all things—the sheep and the cattle and all the wild animals, the birds in the sky, the fish in the sea, and everything that swims the ocean currents.

PSALM 8:6-8

DIVINE DOMINION

Human beings are meant to care for the living things on the earth. In recording the creation of humans, Genesis says, "God blessed them and told them, 'Multiply and fill the earth and subdue it. Be masters over the fish and birds and all the animals'" (Gen. 1:28). In fact, he *brought* each animal directly to Adam. This individual attention shows the value of the animals as well as humankind's dominion over them.

When Jesus Christ, the God-man, was here on earth, he himself demonstrated that dominion. When it was time for Jesus to pay his taxes, he told Peter to cast a hook into the sea. Of all the fish swimming around, the one that bit the hook had a coin in its mouth, and Jesus and Peter used it to pay their taxes (Matt. 17:27). Two times Jesus miraculously multiplied bread and fish so that hungry people could be fed (Matt. 14–15).

Today many humans have, to some degree, strayed from the role God intended us to have with animals. Some people don't give a thought to caring for animals, while others show more care and concern for animals than they do for other people. We are to have an attitude of balanced, caring authority.

How have you cared for the living creatures God has provided for us?

What is man that you should think
of him, and the son of man that you
should care for him? For a little while
you made him lower than the angels,
and you crowned him with
glory and honor.

HEBREWS 2:6-7

Made in God's Image

When God created plants and animals, he called the creation "good." But when he created man and woman, he said, "Let us make people in our image, to be like ourselves" (Gen. 1:26). Later, after Creation, it says, "So God created people in his own image; God patterned them after himself" (verse 27). That means that human beings, unlike plant and animal life, have not only a body but a soul, a mind, emotions, and a will. Unlike plants and animals, man has a God-given spirit.

With your body you know the world beneath you. But with your spirit, you know the world above you. God made us with a spiritual capacity to know him, to love him, and to serve him. We are the distinct creation of almighty God. He made fish with the capacity to swim and birds with the capacity to fly, but he created within man a God-shaped vacuum that can be filled only by the redemption Christ offers through his shed blood on the cross for our sins.

We are, in short, made in God's image, for his glory and purposes. He's always thinking about us because we are near to his heart.

You are the salt of the earth. But what
good is salt if it has lost its flavor? . . .
You are the light of the world—like
a city on a mountain, glowing in
the night for all to see.

MATTHEW 5:13-14

A Salty Christianity

Matthew 5:13 says, "You are the salt of the earth." What is that talking about, in today's terms?

Well, what does salt do? It seasons food to make it more palatable, more interesting, more zippy. As a little boy once said when asked to define salt, "Salt is what tastes bad when you don't have it." How right he was!

God has called Christians to give to life and society a special flavor, a tang, a zest. Yet so many Christians in America are simply living bland lives. There is no excitement, no thrill. Their tasteless, flavorless moments run into days, then the days into years, until all their lifetime is one blah after another.

When you meet a blah person, do you want to spend time with him or her? Probably not, because no one likes to be bored. Even more, would you be tantalized by his or her Christian faith? Definitely not, because you'd be afraid that becoming a Christian would make you bland and uninteresting.

Colossians 4:6 says, "Let your conversation be gracious and effective so that you will have the right answer for everyone." In other words, let your speech and your actions always be seasoned with salt.

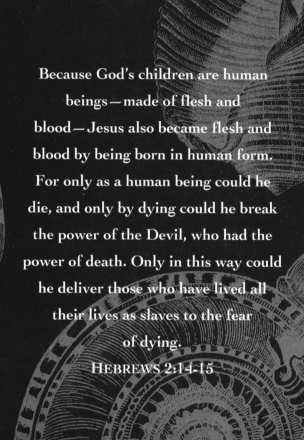

Because God's children are human beings—made of flesh and blood—Jesus also became flesh and blood by being born in human form. For only as a human being could he die, and only by dying could he break the power of the Devil, who had the power of death. Only in this way could he deliver those who have lived all their lives as slaves to the fear of dying.

HEBREWS 2:14-15

Victory through Calvary

During World War II, the rulers of the Western world held a conference in Potsdam. There they wrote out an ultimatum and sent it to Japan. It said in effect: "You must surrender totally and unconditionally. And if you do not surrender, we will destroy your cities, and we will not spare you if you do not surrender."

Japan's response? "We will not surrender. We'll fight on." And they did. As a result, the Americans dropped the atomic bomb so that the Japanese would have to surrender totally and unconditionally.

Christians, too, have an enemy who doesn't want to surrender. The devil continues to fight on, trying to destroy those who believe in Christ in any way he can. Yet at Calvary God dropped an A-bomb on Satan. By rising from the dead, Jesus showed that he alone holds power over death. No longer do we who are Christians have to fear Satan, the master discourager. For when we accept Christ's death on the cross on our behalf, we, too, become victorious through Christ. When Satan comes against us, he runs up against the Jesus who's in us.

In difficult times always remember that you have a powerful friend in high places—and that he, once and for all, has claimed and demonstrated victory over sin and death.

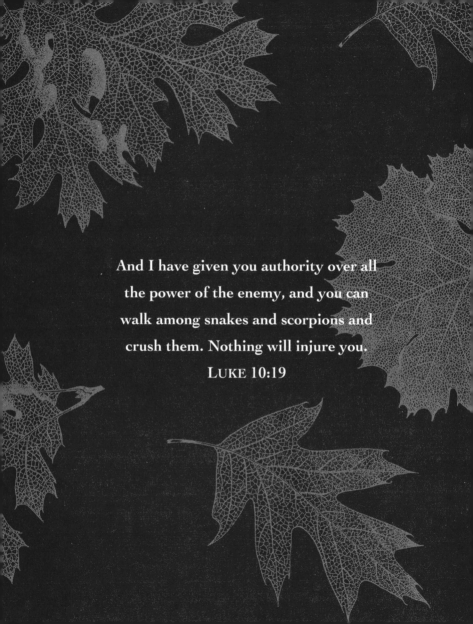

And I have given you authority over all the power of the enemy, and you can walk among snakes and scorpions and crush them. Nothing will injure you.

LUKE 10:19

IN JESUS' NAME

When I was a boy, it was an honor to be involved with my elementary school's "patrol." Everyone looked forward to the day he or she could wear that belt with a badge and help the other boys and girls cross the street. One day they selected me to be a patrol boy. I really looked forward to standing in the street, putting my hand out, and making cars stop. What power, what prestige!

But I wasn't as powerful as I thought I was. The first time I stood out there in the street and held up my hand for a car to stop, the most anticlimatic thing happened: the driver just waved back and drove on. I felt so defeated. But, you see, just holding up my hand wasn't enough. I had to learn to flash my badge of authority along with my hand to make cars stop.

God has given us, as Christians, a badge of authority, too: the name of Jesus Christ. Scripture says that if we ask anything in Jesus' name, within his will, he will do that very thing.

Friends, our Lord has given us authority. The only way the devil can overcome you is if you fail to understand that authority. So the next time you face a difficult circumstance, don't forget: Use the authoritative badge of Jesus' name.

Always be joyful. Keep on praying. No matter what happens, always be thankful, for this is God's will for you who belong to Christ Jesus. . . . Hold on to what is good. Now may the God of peace make you holy in every way, and may your whole spirit and soul and body be kept blameless until that day when our Lord Jesus Christ comes again.

1 THESSALONIANS 5:16-18, 21, 23

HOLDING ON TO HOPE

"In the last days there will be very difficult times. For people will love only themselves and their money. They will be boastful and proud, scoffing at God, disobedient to their parents, and ungrateful. They will consider nothing sacred" (2 Tim. 3:1-2).

These verses, penned so many centuries ago, capture our world today. Friend, it's obvious that we live in dangerous days. The Bible says that Satan is going to come in the last days, and that we're going to see more "miracles" than we've ever seen before. However, most of them will not be accomplished by God; they'll be carried out by the power of Satan—the power of darkness. The Bible even tells us to look for an explosion of the occult. One look at the television, the newsstand, the Internet, etc., will show you that darkness is spreading around our world.

But even in the presence of evil, we don't have to face the rest of our days without hope. God tells us what we must do: "You should keep a clear mind in every situation. Don't be afraid of suffering for the Lord. Work at bringing others to Christ. Complete the ministry God has given you" (2 Tim. 4:5). And, as 1 Thessalonians 5:16 states, we are to "always be joyful"—no matter what comes— remembering who is ultimately in control.

For God so loved the world that he gave his only Son, so that everyone who believes in him will not perish but have eternal life. God did not send his Son into the world to condemn it, but to save it.

JOHN 3:16-17

A GIFT FROM GOD

In the late 1800s and early 1900s, the "Billy Graham" of the day was William Ashley Sunday, known as Billy Sunday. One day, after an evangelistic event, Billy Sunday was helping the workers take down the tent, when a young man came running in. Out of breath, the young man said, "I wanted to come to the revival, but I missed the meeting. But please tell me, what must I do to be saved?"

Sunday simply responded, "You're too late," then kept on taking down the tent.

The young man gasped. "Just because I missed the meeting, you're not going to tell me how to be saved?"

Sunday replied, "No, you're too late to do anything to be saved, because Jesus did it all almost two thousand years ago. Now you *receive* the finished work of Jesus Christ."

How thankful I am for this truth: that upon Jesus' death on the cross, we no longer have to *do* anything. God has offered eternal salvation free of charge through offering his beloved Son for us. There is nothing we can do to earn his love or favor; all we need to do is *receive* it.

Thank God for his precious gift that leads us to everlasting life with him!

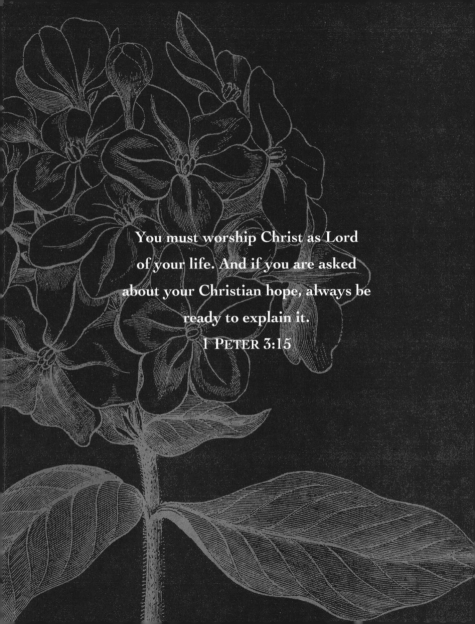

You must worship Christ as Lord of your life. And if you are asked about your Christian hope, always be ready to explain it.

1 PETER 3:15

A READY ANSWER

If you could choose the greatest gift to give someone, what would that be? Would you give a car that runs consistently? a home for a homeless family? peace of mind for someone who's depressed? a pain-free day for someone with a chronic illness?

Nothing can replace the lasting peace or joy that God offers—even in the midst of tough times. So often we're afraid to share with others our "ready answer" for the hope that's within us: Jesus Christ. We wonder if someone will ignore us, argue with us, or—even worse—laugh at us for being "religious." Yet what the world needs the most today is the truth of Christ, for he is the only rock-solid foundation that matters for all eternity.

As the end of all time on earth draws nearer, it's even more crucial that we Christians know who we are, what we believe, and why we believe it. We must not be ashamed of the gospel or of our Lord and Savior, Jesus Christ. This doesn't mean our life as a Christian will always be easy or that people will always listen to us. However, our role is to be the messenger of the Good News—to always be prepared with a ready answer. The rest, including the preparing of the person's heart, is up to God.

We are citizens of heaven, where the
Lord Jesus Christ lives. And we are
eagerly waiting for him to return as
our Savior. He will take these weak
mortal bodies of ours and change them
into glorious bodies like his own, using
the same mighty power that he will use
to conquer everything, everywhere.

PHILIPPIANS 3:20-21

BEAUTIFUL REWARD

One day a country fellow and his family went to town. As he and his sons waited patiently for his wife to finish her shopping "in the big city," he saw something he'd never seen before: an elevator. He stared at its doors for a few minutes, fascinated. Then, suddenly, the doors opened, and a decrepit old woman got on. The door closed, and he watched the dial go up and then come back down. But when the doors opened this time, a beautiful young lady stepped off.

With eyes as big as saucers, he said to his boys, "Sons, you stay right here. I'm going to get your mother and run her through that thing!"

The country fellow thought he was seeing a miraculous transformation. But even if an elevator *could* produce such a transformation (and we know it cannot), it would be nothing compared to what happens when we meet the Lord Jesus Christ in the air. The Bible says he'll change our vile, earthly bodies into glorious heavenly bodies.

So if you don't consider yourself "beautiful" in this life, don't worry. Someday you'll have a glorious body in heaven. What's more—you'll have the opportunity to gather around the throne of God and worship him day and night, without growing weary. Now that's a beautiful reward!

We know how dearly God loves us,
because he has given us the Holy Spirit
to fill our hearts with his love.

ROMANS 5:5

THE BRIDE OF CHRIST

Most every woman dreams of being a bride—of walking down the aisle toward the man of her dreams in a long, flowing gown. Of taking her husband's hand and receiving a kiss as they are announced to be "husband and wife." It is the culmination of years of hoping, wishing, and planning—all begun by the spark of love that comes to fruition in the giving of a ring that symbolizes the longing to be one with another person for a lifetime.

When couples get engaged, they make a "promise" to marry—to belong to the other person even though the marriage has not yet been consummated.

When we receive Christ, we become espoused to Christ. We make a promise that we will set ourselves aside for Christ only—even though the marriage described in Revelation has not yet been consummated. However, when we are saved, we're given something better than a diamond engagement ring. We're given the Holy Spirit as our guard and guide.

That Holy Spirit helps us look forward to the time when we can say with the rest of the church, "Hallelujah! For the Lord our God, the Almighty, reigns. Let us be glad and rejoice and honor him. For the time has come for the wedding feast of the Lamb, and his bride has prepared herself" (Rev. 19:6-7).

You husbands must love your wives with the same love Christ showed the church. He gave up his life for her to make her holy and clean, washed by baptism and God's word. He did this to present her to himself as a glorious church without a spot or wrinkle or any other blemish. Instead, she will be holy and without fault.

EPHESIANS 5:25-27

A WEDDING GIFT

What makes you feel loved? Is it someone who goes out of her way for you? an appreciation note tucked in your lunch? a red rose? a phone call? a surprise weekend getaway?

Couples who truly love each other know that gifts of love must extend beyond the vows they repeat to each other at the altar on their wedding day. Every subsequent action through the years must say, *I'm doing this because I love you. You are the dearest, most precious person to me in the universe, with the exception of our Lord Jesus Christ.*

Listen to what John 13:34 says about loving your spouse: "Love each other. Just as I have loved you, you should love each other." That's a strong statement, since Christ's love for his church is eternally wide and deep. But it's the image God used to show us how much we should love each other—and also a symbol to help us to understand how much God loves us.

How incredible it is that because we are the chosen bride of Christ, we are so dear to our Lord Jesus Christ that he died for us. And even more, he awaits with longing our arrival in heaven, where we can spend time with our Loved One eternally!

Christ is the visible image of the invisible God. He existed before God made anything at all and is supreme over all creation. He existed before everything else began, and he holds all creation together.

COLOSSIANS 1:15, 17

THE REGULATOR

Most of us have at least heard the lyrics of the song "He's Got the Whole Word in His Hands." Actually, those words underestimate God's power. God has the whole wide *universe* in his hands. In fact, he's the Regulator of everything that is, that was, and that will be. Colossians 1:16 says, "Christ is the one through whom God created everything in heaven and earth. He made the things we can see and the things we can't see—kings, kingdoms, rulers, and authorities. Everything has been created through him and for him."

You see, God is the one who spoke everything into existence. Genesis 1:3 states, "Then God said, 'Let there be light,' and there was light." He's the one who created plants, animals, and human-kind. And he's the one who will someday fold up the earth and heavens and tuck them away in the vast drawer of his universe. Revelation 21:1 says, "The old heaven and the old earth had disappeared. And the sea was also gone."

God is the true Regulator of the universe. And because he's the one in charge of all things, we as Christians never need to fear—even when we're faced with bad news. We know the one who holds the stars in his hands.

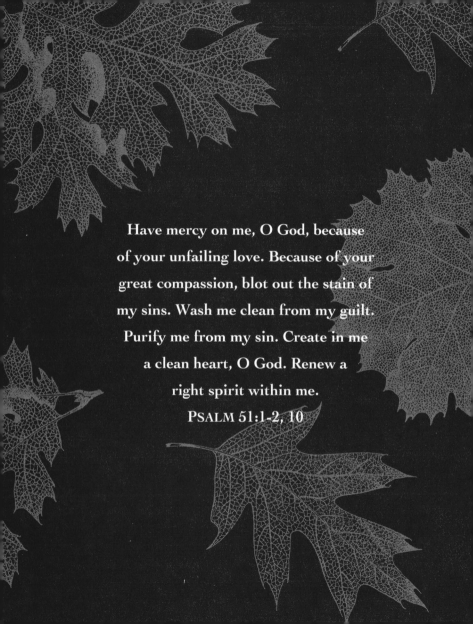

Have mercy on me, O God, because
of your unfailing love. Because of your
great compassion, blot out the stain of
my sins. Wash me clean from my guilt.
Purify me from my sin. Create in me
a clean heart, O God. Renew a
right spirit within me.

PSALM 51:1-2, 10

A GODLY CONSCIENCE

Do you know why some people don't want to attend church, read the Bible, or pray? Because they've offended God in some way, and they have a guilty conscience.

You see, the conscience is the inner judge God has created to help us. It cannot *make* us do right, because God has given us free will. But it shows us what is right and what is wrong. When we do what's right, we feel tremendous relief and freedom. When we do wrong, we suffer.

Just ask David, an Old Testament king. After David had sinned by committing adultery with the beautiful Bathsheba and plotting her husband's death, he said in Psalm 51:3: "I recognize my shameful deeds—they haunt me day and night." Can you imagine what it was like for David to live that way, knowing he had sinned? His sin reverberated constantly through his consciousness. Every time he ran into someone, he probably wondered, "Does this person know?" When a foot messenger arrived with a letter, he probably wondered, "Is this the proof that I'm guilty?" If they'd had a telephone in that day, he probably would have jumped every time it rang.

On the other hand, a good conscience does *good* for you—it allows you a good night's sleep and guilt-free days.

So now, with God as our witness, I give you this charge for all Israel, the Lord's assembly: Be careful to obey all the commands of the Lord your God, so that you may possess this good land and leave it to your children as a permanent inheritance.

1 CHRONICLES 28:8

Celebrating God

If you brought your children up to the front of your church, placed a microphone in front of them, and asked them, "What is the most important thing to your daddy?" and "What is the most important thing to your momma?" what do you think they would say?

I wonder how many children would say, "My dad loves God with all of his heart" or "The most important thing on earth to my momma is her relationship with God and worshiping him."

If we want our children to grow up following and honoring Christ, we must *celebrate* God in front of our children every day—not just on Sunday. That means we make prayer a priority not only at mealtimes but during times of stress, uncertainty, and joy. Our children must see us on our knees, worshiping our heavenly Father. They must be aware that we set aside time not only to read our Bible but to search it for God's will for us. They must walk with us as we marvel at the sunset God created and wonder at the uniqueness of each raindrop or snowflake.

How are you doing on celebrating God in your everyday life? Do your children know the Almighty is your first priority?

No, I will not abandon you as orphans—I will come to you. In just a little while the world will not see me again, but you will. For I will live again, and you will, too.

JOHN 14:18-19

Never Alone

One of the worst things a man can do is father a child and then abandon that child. And yet our world is filled with news stories of exactly that happening: A newborn is left in a garbage can. A mother becomes a single parent because the father doesn't want to take responsibility.

But in such a world, we can be sure of one thing: God brought us into existence, and he will not abandon us—for any reason. He's not concerned about whether it's convenient or not to take care of us. He came to earth in human form to take our sin on his shoulders and then to die for that sin. With his words just before death—"It is finished" (John 19:30)—his work on earth was completed. As a result of his resurrection, there is hope and joy for all who believe in him.

When we give our heart to God, when we trust him as Lord and Savior, he gives us the Holy Spirit to constantly guard and guide us, to protect us, and to care for us. It's the fulfillment of Jesus' promise while we are still on earth that he will never leave us nor forsake us.

You can be assured that the great God who created you will not abandon you—ever.

God bought you with a high price.
So you must honor God.
1 CORINTHIANS 6:20

REMEMBERING OUR CREATOR

If you could list the people you respect the most, whom would you list? Why? Because they've made an impact on your and others' lives? Because they're faithful and honorable? Because you remember the times they've helped you?

Of all the people we should remember and respect most, our Father, God, the almighty Creator, should be first. Genesis 1:1 is a simple presentation of four reasons we should remember God: "In the beginning God created the heavens and the earth." First, God is God, and we should recognize him. Second, God is sovereign and powerful, and we should respect him. Third, God is purposeful, and we should reverence him. Fourth, God is savingly personal—he's a Creator we should acknowledge and trust.

Therefore, the first words of the Bible show us strongly that we have a solemn obligation to remember God. Other Scriptures back up that same foundational truth. For instance, Ecclesiastes 12:1 says, "Don't let the excitement of youth cause you to forget your Creator. Honor him in your youth." And Isaiah 45:9 warns, "Destruction is certain for those who argue with their Creator. Does a clay pot ever argue with its maker?"

Let's not forget we have an obligation to God—he created us and bought us, so we're twice his!

Peter arrived and went inside. He also
noticed the linen wrappings lying
there, while the cloth that had covered
Jesus' head was folded up and lying
to the side. Then the other disciple
also went in, and he saw and
believed — for until then they hadn't
realized that the Scriptures said he
would rise from the dead.

JOHN 20:6-9

THE GREAT ESCAPE

Harry Houdini was such an ingenious escape artist that people thought of all kinds of ways to keep him locked up. Given time, however, he always was able to concoct an escape plan. Sometimes they'd put him in a coffin and bury it. Sometimes they would sew him up in a canvas bag. Sometimes they would seal him in metal milk cans and weld them together—yet somehow he'd always escape.

Yet there came a day when Harry Houdini died—and he did not escape. No skill or trickery could be used. There was no flexibility in the timing. Harry Houdini simply died, and there was nothing he could do about it.

There is only one person who has made the great escape from death—Jesus Christ, the Son of God, who died for our sins and rose again, per his own words, "on the third day" (Matt. 16:21).

When the distraught Mary went to the tomb to anoint Jesus' body with spices, she discovered—at first to her dismay—that his body was missing. She got the apostles stirred up, and they came running to check out the tomb also. Later Mary encountered the living Christ, who had risen from the grave.

Now *that's* a great escape act!

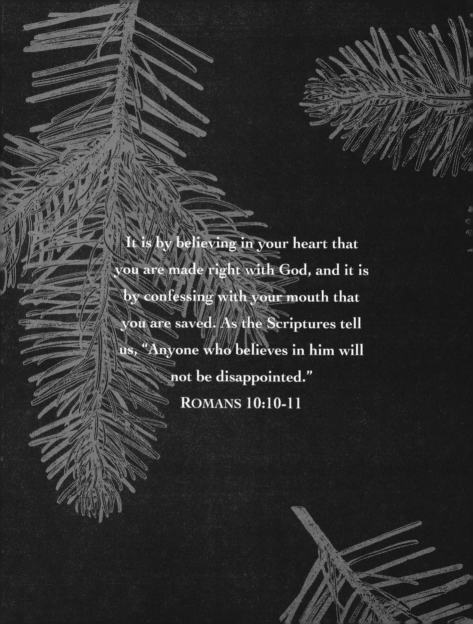

It is by believing in your heart that you are made right with God, and it is by confessing with your mouth that you are saved. As the Scriptures tell us, "Anyone who believes in him will not be disappointed."

ROMANS 10:10-11

THE GIFT OF SALVATION

Have you ever noticed that when you mention Jesus in some circles—even "Christian" ones—there are some who want to change the subject? They begin to look hot and uncomfortable. They barely bow their heads over a meal when you pray in a restaurant; then they pretend they're just rubbing their eyebrow or getting a speck out of their eye when the waiter comes along. When you mention something God has done for you, they mumble some sort of flimsy excuse about needing to leave quickly or spout off, "Hey, what about that ball game last night?" effectively switching channels.

You know why these people are ashamed to be connected with the cause of Christ? Because they don't know what they have in Jesus: the wonderful gift of salvation. They don't realize how important it is to be secure in their eternal future because God raised Jesus from the dead. They don't grasp hold of the supply of boundless spiritual riches available to those who confess Jesus Christ.

How about you? How do *you* react when someone prays in a restaurant? Are you ashamed of Christ, or do you proclaim boldly the gift of his salvation?

Yes, I am the vine; you are the
branches. Those who remain in me,
and I in them, will produce much fruit.
For apart from me you can do nothing.

JOHN 15:5

THE RIGHT CLIMATE

You've seen other factories, but have you ever seen a fruit factory? Not likely, because fruit isn't manufactured in factories; it's grown in orchards.

In the same way, we cannot "manufacture" the fruits of the Spirit, such as kindness and self-control. Instead, we have to be patient in allowing the fruits to ripen and grow throughout our lifetime. The only way we can do that is by walking in the Spirit. Galatians 5:22-23 says, "When the Holy Spirit controls our lives, he will produce this kind of fruit in us: love, joy, peace, patience, kindness, goodness, faithfulness, gentleness, and self-control."

In order for it to grow and ripen, fruit has to be in the right climate. Just as you can't grow bananas in Alaska, you're not going to grow spiritually and produce fruit unless you're abiding in the Spirit. Jesus shows how important that concept is when he says in John 15:4, "Remain in me, and I will remain in you. For a branch cannot produce fruit if it is severed from the vine, and you cannot be fruitful apart from me."

Are you abiding in the Holy Spirit? Are you allowing your fruit to ripen in the right climate?

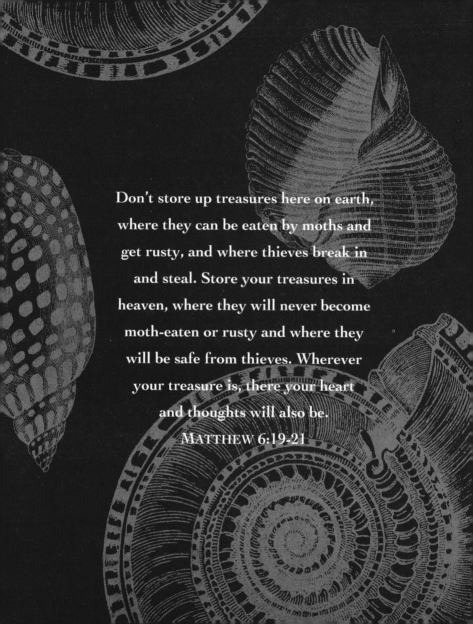

Don't store up treasures here on earth,
where they can be eaten by moths and
get rusty, and where thieves break in
and steal. Store your treasures in
heaven, where they will never become
moth-eaten or rusty and where they
will be safe from thieves. Wherever
your treasure is, there your heart
and thoughts will also be.

MATTHEW 6:19-21

TRUE RICHES

Every day we hear more on the news about the world's troubles and the threat of entire economic systems collapsing.

But for those of us who are Christians, we shouldn't be surprised. The Bible tells us that one day everything that's of this earth will be destroyed. When we realize that truth, earthly wealth is quickly put into perspective. If we want to know how rich we really are, we should add up everything that money cannot buy or that death or disaster can't take away. What's left? Our true riches in Christ Jesus.

If you're constantly worrying about earthly riches, maybe it's time to change your perspective and start to lay up true riches — those that will never perish or fade away. First John 2:15, 17 clearly points the way to a godly perspective on riches: "Stop loving this evil world and all that it offers you, for when you love the world, you show that you do not have the love of the Father in you. And this world is fading away, along with everything it craves. But if you do the will of God, you will live forever."

How much time do you spend in laboring for the riches of this world as compared to piling up riches in heaven? Do you need to reevaluate your life and schedule?

Our High Priest offered himself to God as one sacrifice for sins, good for all time. Then he sat down at the place of highest honor at God's right hand. For by that one offering he perfected forever all those whom he is making holy.

HEBREWS 10:12, 14

Onetime Payment

Do you ever wish God would overlook your "smaller" sins—that little lie you told to keep you out of trouble, the gossip you shared with a friend?

In God's kingdom, there's no hierarchy on sin. God can never overlook any kind of sin. Why? Because God is utterly holy, and by that same holiness he has sworn that sin will be punished. If God were to let one-half of one sin go unpunished, he would no longer be holy.

The Cross is God's way to punish sin and forgive the sinner at the same time by having an innocent, sinless sin-bearer carry the sins of the world to the cross. As 2 Corinthians 5:21 says, "For God made Christ, who never sinned, to be the offering for our sin, so that we could be made right with God through Christ." Jesus Christ suffered the horrors of hell on that cross—he paid for all sins of all people for all time.

Jesus Christ made the ultimate sacrifice—and we only need to accept it on our behalf. As the apostle Paul states in 2 Corinthians 5:20, "We urge you, as though Christ himself were here pleading with you, 'Be reconciled to God!'" Are you reconciled to God?

The love of the Lord remains forever
with those who fear him. His salvation
extends to the children's children of
those who are faithful to his covenant,
of those who obey his commandments!

PSALM 103:17-18

Passing On the Faith

A woman once came to her pastor and asked, "When should I start the religious training of my child? When will he be old enough? Is it too early to start at six years of age?"

Her pastor responded, "No, that's too late."

"But then when should I start?" she queried.

The pastor's simple answer was, "With his grandparents."

What this pastor said is backed by the truths of Scripture. I love what the apostle Paul said to his "dear son" in the Lord, Timothy, in 2 Timothy 1:5: "I know that you sincerely trust the Lord, for you have the faith of your mother, Eunice, and your grandmother, Lois." Isn't that great? Timothy's Christian faith started with his grandma and mother and then was passed on to Timothy himself. What a wonderful heritage of faith!

Just think—since our heritage of faith is passed down, we can live for our grandchildren and great-grandchildren *now*. If we do so, we have the promise of Deuteronomy 7:9: "Understand, therefore, that the Lord your God is indeed God. He is the faithful God who keeps his covenant for a thousand generations."

Whatever you do, you must do all
for the glory of God.
1 CORINTHIANS 10:31

A Spiritual Relationship

If you had to choose which of these events in the life of Jesus was the most "spiritual," what would you say?

- when he preached the Sermon on the Mount
- when he raised Lazarus from the dead
- when he washed his disciples' feet
- when he spat on the ground and made mud to anoint the blind man's eyes

The actual answer is *none:* they were *all* equally spiritual. Jesus did not segment life into "more spiritual" and "less spiritual." He did everything with the purpose of glorifying his Father: "I brought glory to you here on earth by doing everything you told me to do" (John 17:4).

If you acted on this philosophy—of viewing everything you do (feeding your baby, driving to work, interacting with friends, cooking dinner) as a spiritual activity instead of just a regular part of your day—how would your perspective change?

As we incorporate our faith into real life, others will notice. As John 17:22-23 says, "I have given them the glory you gave me, so that they may be one, as we are—I in them and you in me, all being perfected into one. Then the world will know that you sent me and will understand that you love them as much as you love me." What a wonderful testimony!

I am the living one who died. Look, I
am alive forever and ever! And I hold
the keys of death and the grave.

REVELATION 1:18

THE RISEN CHRIST

It's interesting how history honors people in the past tense.

When my wife and I were in Moscow, I told her, "We cannot leave Moscow without seeing Lenin's tomb." So we went to the Kremlin to view it in all its glory. Lenin, a Russian Communist leader, is sealed carefully in a crystal case so that he can be visited by the Russian people—and curious tourists like us. His face is waxen. His beard is perfectly trimmed. And his case is protected by soldiers standing stoically nearby.

But what struck us most were the words on his tombstone: "He was the greatest leader of all peoples of all countries of all times. He was the lord of the new humanity. He was the Savior of the world." And yet there lies that dead dictator. Do you notice the words are all past tense? He *was*.

But Jesus said, "I am the living one who died. I am alive forever and ever!" Friend, I want to tell you that makes all the difference. It is an encounter with the living Christ that convinces people who he really is—the Son of God, the true Savior of the world, the risen Christ.

If my people who are called by my name will humble themselves and pray and seek my face and turn from their wicked ways, I will hear from heaven and will forgive their sins.

2 CHRONICLES 7:14

A DYNAMITE FAITH

Suppose someone came up to you and, for no reason, punched you in the nose — *Pow!* — with his big fist. And just suppose that afterward, in an act of Christian compassion (after you got up from the ground with your head spinning), you said to that person, "I forgive you."

What if that person then responded, "There's no need for you to forgive me. I've already forgiven myself"?

Although this situation may be highly unlikely, it's got a poignant point: Only the punch-ee can forgive the puncher. When it comes to our own sin before God, we are the punchers, and God is the punch-ee. When we clench our fist before the face of God, only he can forgive our sin.

What was the reason for the Cross? *Sin.* "Christ also suffered when he died for our sins once for all time. He never sinned, but he died for sinners that he might bring us safely home to God. He suffered physical death, but he was raised to life in the Spirit" (1 Pet. 3:18). There's enough gospel dynamite in that one verse to blow the sin, the hatred, the sorrow, and the sickness out of anybody's life, but it must first be ignited by the spark of faith.

The Lord himself will come down from heaven with a commanding shout, with the call of the archangel, and with the trumpet call of God. First, all the Christians who have died will rise from their graves. Then, together with them, we who are still alive and remain on the earth will be caught up in the clouds to meet the Lord in the air and remain with him forever.

1 THESSALONIANS 4:16-17

ANTICIPATING HIS COMING

We live in strange days—abortion, human cloning, rampant disease, school shootings, rising numbers of rapes and murders. With such evil and fatalistic philosophies abounding, it's no wonder people are predicting the end of the world.

However, so many people get wrapped up in the details of prophesying that they fail to anticipate the person who's coming: Jesus Christ. The core difference between false cults and true Christians is that false cults tell you to *believe something*. Christians tell you to *receive someone*—the Lord Jesus.

When all these horrible things come to pass, they should grieve and sadden us but not shake us. Why? Because we know God's Word—and the end of the human story. As Jesus said, "Then everyone will see the Son of Man arrive on the clouds with power and great glory. So when all these things begin to happen, stand straight and look up, for your salvation is near!" (Luke 21:27-28).

When I think about Jesus, the Son of God, coming to earth again, I get excited. I want to shout with the hymn writer Horatio Gates Spafford, "And, Lord, haste the day when the faith shall be sight, the clouds be rolled back as a scroll, the trump shall resound and the Lord shall descend, 'even so'—it is well with my soul."

Since everything around us is going to melt away, what holy, godly lives you should be living! You should look forward to that day and hurry it along — the day when God will set the heavens on fire and the elements will melt away in the flames.

2 PETER 3:11-12

The Wonderful Wedding

Aren't weddings wonderful—the flowers, the glowing candles, the emotion of the ceremony and lifetime vows exchanged, the loveliness of the bride in her flowing gown, the radiant face of the groom, the smiles and happy tears of the guests? All of these elements combine to make the event indescribably thrilling.

God knew what he was doing when he chose a wedding to describe to us that moment when we become totally and eternally one with the Lord Jesus Christ—when he takes us with him to live in heaven forever. The book of Revelation calls it "the wedding feast of the Lamb" (Rev. 19:7) and describes it as being incredibly exciting to finally become intimately one with our God in reality, for all time.

When we're swept up to meet the Lord in glory and we meet him face-to-face, what bliss that will be! And when we become one with him in a union that's so fulfilling nothing on this earth could touch it, our heavenly marriage will finally be consummated.

As Scripture says, "We are looking forward to the new heavens and new earth he has promised, a world where everyone is right with God" (2 Pet. 3:13). Now that's a wedding you don't want to miss!

All praise to him who loves us and has
freed us from our sins by shedding
his blood for us. He has made us his
Kingdom and his priests who serve
before God his Father. Give to him
everlasting glory! He rules
forever and ever! Amen!

REVELATION 1:5-6

CROWNING THE KING

Last week my wife, Joyce, and I did something we haven't done for years: we got out our checkerboard. After we had played for a while, I spotted a great move. I skipped my man into King's Row and announced triumphantly, "Crown me!"

That move is not unlike what's going to happen when Jesus Christ comes again. Right now the kingdoms of this world are being moved around like checkers, and the game has not yet ended. But soon God's going to place his Son into King's Row and say, "Crown him."

What should we, as Christians, do in the meantime? We can pray with all our heart what Jesus taught us to pray in Matthew 6:10: "May your Kingdom come soon. May your will be done here on earth, just as it is in heaven."

As we look at the crimes all around us—rape, incest, murder, child abuse—we may shake our head in horror, saying, "That's certainly not God's will." But someday God's will *will* be done on earth, when he comes again. That will be the day God puts his King upon the holy hill of Zion, and all humankind will bow before him.

Are you looking forward to the day when God will shout with glorious triumph, "It's time! Crown him King!"?